ADVANCE PRAISE FOR
Scam Goddess

"Laci Mosley is a hilarious and wise rule breaker and Scam Goddess reminds you there are many ways to 'live your dream.'"

—AMY POEHLER

"Laci could scam me into anything (like writing this blurb). Laci always makes me laugh and this book is no different."

—CONAN O'BRIEN

"Laci scammed me into to writing this! Kidding. Laci is one of the funniest, most incisive people I know, and this book has all the wit and heart I've come to expect as her friend. This book ain't a scam, it's a joy."

—IRA MADISON III,
HOST OF *KEEP IT* AND
AUTHOR OF *PURE INNOCENT FUN*

"One of the funniest books I've ever read. . . .
Laci is the beautiful and the scammed as she navigates a
world trying to keep everyone down, with laugh-a-millisecond
honesty and empathy for the people frauding for good.
I now have my next ten scams planned and ready.
Thank you, Goddess."

"This whole book is a scam.
It distracts you with constant laughter but you're
actually learning valuable life lessons and falling
deeper and deeper in love with its author."

Scam Goddess

Lessons from a Life of Cons, Grifts, and Schemes

Lessons from
a Life of Cons,
Grifts, and Schemes

Scam Goddess

Laci Mosley

RUNNING PRESS
PHILADELPHIA

Text copyright © 2024 by Laci Mosley
Cover photograph © 2022 by Brett Erickson
Cover copyright © 2024 by Hachette Book Group, Inc.

Running Press
Hachette Book Group
1290 Avenue of the Americas, New York, NY 10104
www.runningpress.com
@Running_Press

First Edition: September 2024

Published by Running Press, an imprint of Hachette Book Group, Inc. The
Running Press name and logo are trademarks of Hachette Book Group, Inc.

The Hachette Speakers Bureau provides a wide range of authors for
speaking events. To find out more, go to www.hachettespeakersbureau.com
or email HachetteSpeakers@hbgusa.com.

Running Press books may be purchased in bulk for business, educational,
or promotional use. For more information, please contact your local
bookseller or the Hachette Book Group Special Markets Department
at Special.Markets@hbgusa.com.

Print book interior design by Amanda Richmond
Print book cover design by Jack Smyth

Library of Congress Cataloging-in-Publication Data
Names: Mosley, Laci, author.
Title: Scam goddess : lessons from a life of cons, grifts, and schemes /
Laci Mosley.
Description: First edition. | Philadelphia : Running Press, 2024. |
Includes bibliographical references.
Identifiers: LCCN 2024000716 | ISBN 9780762484652 (hardcover) |
ISBN 9780762484676 (ebook)
Subjects: LCSH: Mosley, Laci. | Podcasters--United States--Biography. |
Swindlers and swindling--Biography. | LCGFT: Essays. | Humor.
Classification: LCC PN4587.2.M67 A3 2024 |
DDC 791.46092 [B]--dc23/eng/20240327
LC record available at https://lccn.loc.gov/2024000716

ISBNs: 978-0-7624-8465-2 (hardcover), 978-0-7624-8467-6 (ebook)

Printed in the United States of America

LSC-C

Printing 1, 2024

I have to start this dedication
by thanking God, aka my mother,
Lori Bishop, for letting me scam her out of
her body's resources in the womb. Pregnancy
is crazy, y'all—did you know you could lose
teeth? Your nipple could fall off! You could
birth a child who wants to be an actor!? Only
one of those things happened to my mom, and
I'm so grateful that she poured her life, love,
and savvy ways into me. To my grandmother
(I just know they got ebooks in heaven by now),
thank you for scamming me into loving myself.
And to Isaac, I love you daddy.

Contents

INTRODUCTION

I went missing when I was five. Lol.

The day I went missing started off like they all do, with me running the shower and getting clean for the day. I was always an adult-kid hybrid. Even at five, I would shower on my own, and my mom would just give me a quick sniff to make sure I was clean. She had taught me how to bathe well: *Don't use the same towel you use on your body on your face. Wash behind your ears. Don't forget your neck and your belly button.* (We're Black so legs and other extremities were a given.) After my shower, while my mom was getting ready for work, I'd hop on the sink and brush my teeth—just two girlies getting ready for their jobs. At the time, my only job was figuring out how to get my mom to fund my dreams of becoming a performer. Well, that and going to kinder-garten, but I cared more about performing.

Ever since getting my first laugh at a family reunion that summer, I'd become addicted to the sound of laughter. Then, when my family started going on about how funny I was, how I was a natural-born performer, I knew I'd found the thing I wanted to do with my life. It takes a certain amount of delulu (delusion) to want to enter the entertain-ment industry, and I'm lucky that I was born mildly crazy.

I had no fear as a kid. Spending summers on a sprawling country road where your neighbors are also your family members and everyone loves each other gives you a sense of unflappable stability. I miss those days. The beginning stages of any dream is where the fun is. It's all potential. Potential is sexy. It's this thing we love in ourselves and other people.

I had a lot of potential as a kid, and I wanted to utilize that potential. As soon as I realized performing was my calling, I sat my mom down and calmly explained that the natural next step, in my opinion, was to move to Hollywood. Reminder, I was in kindergarten, sooo my mom was like, "Hell no. I'm not going to drive you around to auditions, live out of my car, and make my life all about you." *Um, okay Mom.* It was clear that if I wanted something in this world, I'd have to figure out how to get it on my own. I knew my mom was too resolute to be broken down by the traditional little kid whining, so I had to get creative . . . I gamed the system. In my mom's house, there was basically only one rule, and that rule was that I had to do well in school. So even at five, I made school my number one priority, and because of this, my mom began to reward me with acting workshops: one of the greatest child-exploitation scams.

I personally do not think children should be employed, especially in the business I work in. Parents of child actors are fucking weirdos, and you can quote me on that. I work with child actors—a lot of them—and there's only one family that's not absolutely bizarre. (You know who you are, or maybe you don't . . . That's the point.) These people are willing to throw away their money and move into weird children acting encampments in LA hoping their kid will become the next Zendaya. It makes the child actor industry ripe for scamming because you have these crazed parents trying to will themselves into fame and fortune through their children. In these workshops, it's hard to tell whether what you're doing is actually getting somewhere or whether your kids suck. No one ever gives you a straight answer.

You want to know if your kid has talent? Ask a Black person. Black people always speak the truth. Sure, I learned things from those classes, and my mom managed to maintain healthy boundaries, but I feel like I am a rare case.

So school wasn't just *school* for me; it was an opportunity to unlock all of my acting dreams. Every morning when I'd grab my school folder off the table, filled with teacher notes and post-curricular writing exercises my mom would make me do for some of that extra home learning, I'd shake with the excitement of possibility. If I brought any good news home, I'd get to go to another acting workshop.

On some days, if my mom was going in early to work, her forgettable husband Mr. Tim would drop me off. Seriously, y'all, this guy was just background in my life. I never paid much attention to Mr. Tim because it all went to my mom. Maybe I should've, though, because the day I went missing was a Mr. Tim day. As I walked toward the big glass double doors of Akin Elementary, ready for learning with my blue uniform perfectly pressed, I noticed a white sheet of paper taped to the door. It was high above my head and the writing was too small to read—plus, I was five, so my reading was a work in progress anyway. I ignored the sign, hooked my little baby hand through the handle, and leaned back. Nothing. I pulled a little harder, but still . . . nothing. The door wouldn't budge. Then I noticed it: the quiet. I turned around only to see that the school grounds were completely empty. Not a single soul around . . . not even Mr. Tim, who had dropped me off and skrrt-skrrted away the second my feet had hit the pavement. Damn, you couldn't wait to see if I got inside? Even Uber drivers do that. One star, Stepdaddy Tim.

I turned back around and peeked through the glass windows only to see the hallways were empty too. If I had been tall enough, maybe a whole six years old, I would've been able to see that the sign said the school was closed for a three-day weekend. This was in an era when schools didn't use their websites and parents didn't necessarily check their emails, so they sent kids home with notes and schedules like little carrier pigeons. But just like carrier pigeons, five-year-olds have small brains and short attention spans. I'm sure my note was still sitting in my folder, exactly where my kindergarten teacher, Ms. April, had left it the Friday before. In my defense, I was a good student, eager to please, so when Ms. April had told me there was an important note for my parents in there, I had eagerly shoved my folder in the face of the first adult I saw: Mr. Tim. I'm sure he thought it was another gold star on a four-word spelling test and didn't even bother opening the damn thing.

Basically, I was fucked.

Now, some five-year-olds might've sat on the steps of the school, waiting for an adult to save them. But not me. Nuh-uh. I wasn't about to be a sitting duck, just waiting for an abductor to come get me; I had watched enough *Dateline* with my grandma to know they didn't look for missing Black girls. I had to stay on the move. A little kid with my charisma and adorable button nose? Yeah, I'd be snatched in a minute. I gripped my backpack straps in my hands and marched off of school premises, headed straight back to my apartment.

The old saying goes "everything is bigger in Texas," and from a young age, I was always determined to be the biggest I could be. I carried myself as if I owned any place I stepped into, so it's no wonder people didn't seem to be alarmed by the sight of a five-year-old businesslady roaming the streets unattended—those were *my* streets! When I got to my apartment complex a few blocks away, I felt a pang of relief—it wasn't in my nature to break rules and misbehave. I was what is known as a Good Kid. I went to church, loved school, and was completely uninterested in disobeying my all-seeing mother. My mom didn't allow me to do anything out of her sight unless it was school related. I couldn't even sleep over anywhere because she was like, "I've seen the movies. I don't need you getting murdered by some angry dad." I wasn't sheltered out of closed-mindedness or anything like that; I was sheltered out of protection. My mom knew my safety was ensured in three places: her house, my grandparents' house, and school.

Even though I loved spending time with my family, I was hungry to see more of the world. I was really intrigued by how other people lived because all I'd ever really known was my own little life in the guts of suburban Texas. The only time I wasn't under the strict supervision of a family member was when I was at school. So later on I found a loophole: a way to break the rules while making it look like I was following them. I began signing up for after-school activities, because *technically,* that was still school. I joined the student council. Then I became student council president *and* class president. Then I joined track, the volleyball team, cheerleading, and, of course, theater. I did everything in my power to stay out in the world, learning, absorbing, making friends, doing things. Extracurriculars would become my portal to the great unknown beyond my mother's boundaries. Being in theater became a way to ingratiate myself with the very people I was so curious about.

So yeah—wandering around Texas on my own as a five-year-old was not really my MO. Even though I wasn't technically breaking any rules or doing anything bad, it felt wrong to be outside of school during the day with no supervision. I didn't think on it too much, though, because, again, I was *five.*

I walked past a leasing office, the tennis courts, and the pool to the front door of my place and knocked. Now, okay, yes, if you're a grown-up reading this, then you'll already be like, "Laci, you know no one's gonna be home. It's the beginning of the workday. Protect those little knuckles, girl." But it took me a few minutes, many knocks, and then a few more minutes to realize no one was home.

At this point, getting abducted began to sound more appealing to me. So I set off to do just that: get abducted. I was already giving my best JonBenét, looking *real* milk-carton, national newsworthy in my little blue uniform with the pleated skirt. I know they don't look for Black girls, but with that fit and my big brown eyes? I was hoping they'd at least *pretend*. "Laci Mosley"? Come on. Even my name is cute.

There was a park next to my school, so I figured I'd start there. As soon as I arrived, I saw the perfect targets: two little white kids with their Mexican nanny. Yes, bitch! They were going to make incredible abductors/new family members. We could go home together and have a great life as a perfect American family: two little white children, a Mexican lady, and a Black girl. I puffed up my chest, put on my brightest smile, and walked right up to the kids. "Hi, can I play with you?" Confident. Bold. In control. A good opening line. Could've used an introduction, but kids don't have that kind of etiquette yet. The kids instantly knew I was their adopted sister and acquiesced. I was thrilled. A new family!

We ran across the gravel and began climbing up the stairs to the slide. The whole time, I was giving them compliments—you know, it's the Libra rising in me. I was all, "I love your shirt. I love those sneakers, do they light up? Y'all are so cute! Where did you get that dinosaur shirt? Ooh, is that dress Oshkosh?! Loves!" I was making them feel good about themselves. "I love your haircut. Is it from a bowl?" Even at five, I knew that kindness and compliments could unlock a whole new world for you. Little ol' manipulative me. Little did anyone know. A bitch was missing! I was low-key *missssssinnggg*. Sure, I hadn't made the news yet, but I was missing! Isn't that what missing means?

After a few minutes (or hours?) of playing—I really had no sense of how time worked at that age, and to be honest, I am not too familiar with that bitch in these post-pandemic days either—the nanny stood up and told the kids to get ready to leave. Oh, yeah, the nanny. I centered my focus on her. This was who I really needed to impress, not these dumb kids. I needed the nanny to be my protector, my new mom. So I walked up her to and said, "¿Puedes llevarme contigo?"

Yeah, that's right! I speak Spanish. Bet you didn't see that coming. Most people register subtly racist surprise when they find out that I, a Black person, am bilingual because I had Latina nannies growing up. When you're Black, people assume you come from the worst socio-economic background. They're like, "Wait, how did you get that nanny-money so we can stop that from happening again?" Even today, in expensive spaces, I get a lot of, "What do you do for a living?" aka "How did you get in here?" I always tell people I work in insurance. It sounds boring so there's never a follow-up question. (I'm sure you insurance people live spicy lives, but that's on you for keeping it a secret. Also, thank you for that!) So yes, I grew up with nannies and my nannies spoke Spanish. My first word was *manzana*, apple. I'm a bilingual baddie, moving on.

The lady took one look at me and said, "No." Clearly uninterested in being responsible for another kid. Shit. Okay. With the threat of losing my only contacts in my new life, I got desperate and switched tactics. "Ayúdame por favor. Llama 911." When she heard that, the nanny scooped up the kids and took off, leaving me alone again. I don't blame her for getting the fuck outta there; a lot of the childcare workers in Texas did not have their papers so they were . . . uh . . . not friends with las policías. I get it: I'm not either!

With the sun growing hot and the park completely empty, I decided to try to get in touch with my mom. I'd enjoyed a taste of a nomadic life with my fake park family, but I was getting tired and hungry. Luckily, my aunt and uncle lived in the apartment complex across from ours, so I decided to head their way.

On my way to my aunt and uncle's, I walked by the leasing office, where a small group of people was gathered. One of them, a man, came in hot with a, "Hey, little girl, where are your parents?" It felt harsh and accusatory. I did not like this person's tone. So I screamed at the top of my lungs, flapped my hands at my sides like a little hummingbird, and sprinted in the other direction. If you think this is a weird-ass way to react to people who could potentially get me out of a bad situation, then you're completely right. But unfortunately, at the time, the adults in my life were a mixed bag when it came to help and harm. In that moment, I sensed danger, so I screamed, flapped my wings, and flew away.

I kept running and running until I hit the busy road separating my spot from my aunt and uncle's apartment. At that point, I'd only driven over with my mom, and crossing a six-lane street with a median was definitely above my pay grade as an unemployed freeloader. (That's what I call children.) This is Texas, mind you; our speed limits are like 85 mph so people do a casual 90. But I knew if I could just get to the island in the middle of the lanes, I'd probably be able to make it to the other side. I looked both ways and booked it, hoping not to end up like that little Frogger guy. I'm happy to report that I made it not only to the island, but safely to my aunt and uncle's side of the freeway. They, of course, were not home either. I was somehow smart enough to try to con my way into a white family, get out of a sticky situation at the leasing office, and cross the freeway, but as an unemployed freeloader, I didn't understand the concept of "9 to 5" as anything but a bop by a beautiful big-boobed white lady on the radio.

I got back to the road and prepared for another game of Frogger. This time, I didn't make it all the way across— because a car stopped and the driver asked me to get inside . . . so I did. (Oh my God, don't worry, I'm clearly fine. Can you imagine if I died in the intro of my memoir?) I didn't make it across the freeway because the driver was Ms. April, my teacher.

I cannot tell you how happy my jobless ass was when that car screeched to the side of the median and I heard Ms. April's queenly Black-lady voice call out, "LACI?!?!?!" To look up and see an adult I not only knew but revered was so clutch because at that point in my being-lost-ness, I literally would've gotten into a car with *anyone* who asked. I'm actually kind of shocked nobody tried to abduct me for real. I was very abductable!

Ms. April drove me in her beat-up stick shift (see, she *was* clutch!) to the nearest police-type security station. Or . . . I think it was a police-type security station. I don't *actually* remember where we went or what kind of car Ms. April was driving. I was *five.* When it comes to stories from my childhood, I may have to embellish with some artistic writerly specifics. But all the important details are crystal clear in my mind. You can even google the locations; I'm not scamming you!

What I remember about the station is: I didn't get police vibes but rather major *Paul Blart: Mall Cop* realness from the situation. At the time, I only knew one phone number and that was my mom's. (In fact, that's still the only number I know . . . and she's since changed it, so that's a problem for me.) Next thing I knew, my mom rushed through the doors, absolutely sobbing. The whole experience is seared in my mind for many reasons, but my mom's tears are one of the biggest. She's not much of a crier, and seeing her shook to her core stayed with me. I laud Lori: she's the altar I pray to, the human I hope to be, her pain is my pain, her joy is my joy, and she treats me the same. So in that moment, my adult-five-year-old self decided to be brave, spare her the details of the day (I did spill to my granny later, though, lmao), and confidence myself through the fear once again. I could sense how horrible she felt (even though it wasn't her fault) and how scared she was, and I knew that this was my opportunity to get the one thing I wanted most in life: sugar for dinner. "Mama," I said into her ear as she held my head against her shoulder, rocking back and forth. "Can I have a peanut butter and jelly sandwich for dinner?" I got the sandwich. And shortly after that, my mom and Mr. Tim divorced.

This very true story (I have receipts) came to the forefront of my consciousness shortly after I finished writing the first draft of this book. It's been bouncing around in my head for days—with me when I fall asleep and there when I wake up. Because the day I went missing is the day I began relying on my confidence to survive in the world. This is my very first memory of looking at the cards I was dealt and thinking, *Nope! We can do better!* I didn't know it then, but I see now that I was building my scammer tool kit. Studying the people around me to learn how to con them into giving me those peanut butter and jelly sandwiches. I didn't always get it right—the nanny didn't abduct me (or help me) despite my best efforts—but I had these ingrained instincts. Speaking "Nice White Lady" to the nice, white kids and then switching to perfect Spanish for the Spanish-speaking nanny are a pretty good con if you ask me, especially for a five-year-old.

The day I went missing, I found my path. A path of scams, cons, and frauds. Little ones. Ones that didn't hurt people or get me in trouble. But still ones that would get me to where I needed to be. You see . . . everyone's a scammer and everything's a scam. Some people are better at it than others, but we all do it. Scamming gets a bad rap. *Fraud, scam, con*—all those words have negative connotations, but that's some straight-up bullshit. Being born is a scam! No one asked to be alive. You drop into this world, spend your time figuring out how to be a human, and then, just when you're starting to get the hang of it, you die, which seems really shitty. I certainly didn't ask to be born, yet here I am trying to figure out whether coffee-cup lids are recyclable and why my AirPods keep disconnecting from my phone.

I've always been attracted to scams and cons because the system wasn't built for people like me, so I had to learn how to operate in a way that's most advantageous to me, myself, and I. The problem is: I have a conscience and anxiety, paired with an unshakable desire to people-please. I'm working on it, but it's not an easy toxic trait to dump. And yes, it is toxic. We people-pleasers aren't heroes. Ours is a self-harming form of control that often sprouts from a childhood of conditional love. "If they need me, they won't leave me" ain't cute, and when you say yes to things you don't want to do, you're saying no to yourself. But I digress . . . back to the point: If I'd been a people-pleaser who wasn't also obsessed with scams, I probably would've ended up married to a person I didn't love, with kids I didn't want, in a life I didn't need. Scamming saved me and has taught me how to navigate a messy and unfair world while looking out for myself, too.

This is why I love confidence artists—people who are so secure in themselves that they have no problem wringing exactly what they want and need out of every situation. They are satisfied with just being in the moment, not deep worrying about how the other person is thinking or feeling . . . like people-pleasers do. Con artists aren't scared of failing, losing it all, and losing the affection of those around them. If they were, they couldn't run their scams.

That's something I struggle with: I'm constantly in my head about everything. (Yeah, yeah, I know. Anxiety.) Even though I love a good party, I often find myself lingering at the entrance, stressing out at the thought of being around people, being out there in the world. Solitude is my safe space. Living that soft life with candles, ice cream, no one to please other than myself is a lot easier than being so extra all the time. When you bring other people into the equation, things get complicated.

As a super, hyperinvolved student, I learned to live a transactional type of lifestyle—someone always wanted something out of me and I always needed something out of them. Now, as an overly ambitious adult, I feel like if I don't have something to offer people, they won't like me. That's why I always make sure I have something to offer—a laugh, emotional support, trips, flights, money. I have a bad people-pleasing thing, not good for my personal life, but *great* for acting. My career depends on my ability to please people. The performer-audience relationship is the easiest one for me to figure out: I give you a good time; you give me a good time. And performing really is a good time for me. Hosting a podcast or being in movies or TV is a highly structured time with cues, scripts, editing, and perfect lighting. Living a bold, but highly structured, Hollywood life gives me a chance to be in the world, around people, without the anxiety of being **in** the world, **around** people.

As an actor, comedian, and podcaster, I have no problem projecting confidence. That's why my career is my biggest scam. I *love* performing confidence. I can't tell you how many people meet me and are like, "Bitch, take a seat. You need to be more insecure. You have too much confidence." But it's all just a ruse, a scam. I can play a con artist, and play her well, but the reality is, behind closed doors, I am just a human who is soft and vulnerable, too.

Scamming is truly an art. That's why they're called scam *artists*. These people have costumes. Sometimes they do accents. They're out there putting on a show 24/7. They are true performers. They're mirroring people around them, cosplaying empathy, pretending to be human, when in reality they're impenetrable aliens with zero feelings or concerns. Believe me: it's not easy; I've tried. But I have to say, my favorite thing about scam artists is that they make up all the rules of their world. I love that for them. I love that for me. I love that for us. Scam artists remind us that *we made this all up!* We decided, as a society, how things should function and then created a bunch of laws to make sure things keep functioning that way. And when I say "we," I mean old white dudes.

Everyone knows America was built on scams. We became an economic powerhouse providing two-thirds of the world's cotton by scamming (enslaving) my ancestors. And the same old white dudes who set that up got together and made up all these laws. Why couldn't I have been there to put in my two cents? Seems unfair. I was class president! I love planning! Why didn't all y'all white dudes tag me in?

I wanna make up some of my own laws! Like:

- Everyone should be allowed to be seven minutes late to absolutely everything, even their own funerals.

- If you get towed twelve times in one year, you get a prize for keeping the people at Hollywood Tow Service Inc. in business.

- You're allowed to lie about an illness to get out of something once a month.

- You can't ask people to BYOB if your neighborhood has shit parking. (I have to get an Uber *and* a bottle? You're wild.)

- If you have a destination wedding, you can't ask for gifts. My presence is your present!

- People who own fish should be on a watch list. Who wants a pet you can't cuddle? We know you're a murderer.

- We should be able to steal a little from self-checkout. If you're going to make me work at this Kroger, I'm taking my wages.

- No one should have to pick anyone up from the airport. Ever. Unless you're picking *me* up, in which case, thank you so much. I will never return the favor!

- If you're going to post a sexy pic, you can't caption it with a motivational speech. Why are you quoting Maya Angelou? We're looking at your ass!

- Everyone should know their zodiac sign. And tell it to me immediately so I can decide if I hate you.

These are rules I can get behind, but the rules we have here in America? The laws that have been enforced on us, both written and unwritten? I just can't fuck with them. I'm a dark-skinned Black lady, so you *know* these laws weren't made for my benefit.

This is precisely why I live, breathe, eat, and drink scams up. Scammers were born into a world with a set of rules that they actively *choose* to ignore. They were handed lives they didn't quite fit into, or situations that they hated, and set out to change those lives and situations. That's what I did, too. I didn't want to be lost in Texas, where no one knew who I was or where I was. I never wanted to feel like I was missing again. So I dove into scamming. I made sure no one I met ever forgot my face or name, and it's been a wild ride ever since. If scammers can do it, so can you. And you should—because at the end of the day, everything is a scam and everyone's a scammer. Actors and directors. Award shows. Politicians. Taxes. C-suite executives. Subscription-based services. Tech bros. Cryptocurrency. Writers. This book. It's all just a bunch of people trying to use each other to feel protected from the world, and that's not always a bad thing.

When I first got the opportunity to do a podcast, I knew there was only one topic I could talk about ad nauseam for the rest of my life . . . You guessed it: SCAMS. I'd never done a podcast before and had no clue what I was doing. But like everything in my life, I approached the opportunity with confidence and enthusiasm. I put on my cute little con-artist hat, batted my eyelashes, and said, "Where do I sign?" Well, guess the fuck what? *Scam Goddess* is now an industry-respected, highly popular, award-winning podcast under both the Earwolf and Team Coco banners. Scammed my way into getting paid to talk about scamming. What a racket! Now, it's my time to share my hard-earned good fortune with you, my *congregation*. So, in these pages, you'll find three main topics: (1) the wildest true-crime scams I've ever come across; (2) my own stories of navigating all the sneaky, systemic scams that infect everythinggg; and (3) lessons my independent studies at ScamU have taught me about life.

Like I said, it's a scam being born. None of us chose this for ourselves. (My *mom* didn't even choose my being born. As she likes to jokingly-not-so-jokingly remind me, she unplanned me!) But I'm gonna make the best of it. My life of being a Scam Goddess has led me on a fully unhinged path, a local carnival ride where it's fun and dangerous and sometimes operated by stoned teenagers. And you're going to read about it. All of it. From being caught in the middle of a shootout to getting held hostage on a remote island. Regardless of whether I was sneaking into Beyoncé's VIP section or doing bookkeeping for a drug front—all stories I'll get into—I walked away from every situation empowered, entertained, and genuinely excited to be alive on this earth thanks to my scammer brain and my mama. Remember— she *chose* to let me squat in her body for nine months.

I want the same for you. (Not a parasite you house for eighteen years, unless that's your jam—I mean my make-your-own-rules freedom.) So let's link arms and con our way to the top of the pops.

Yes, everything is a scam, and this book is too, but the stories in it are real, they're funny, and they're written for anyone who needs a little more con(fidence) in their life. The friendship we'll forge will be real, too; you see me, and I see you. That's the beauty of this whole scamming game. If everything's made up, then we can choose what kind of world we live in. I choose a world of humor, light, and fewer parking tickets. What do you choose?

Religious Scams

Some scams are easy for me to digest. Others go down like a blazing swig of Hennessey. The absolute racket that *is* organized religion is one of those throat-burning ones. Even though I have no problem speaking critically about organized religion, I still feel a deep connection to the powers that be. Church has always played a big role in my life. It shaped me as a kid. These days, though, I consider myself more of a Bedside Baptist. I go to church for the major holidays because they're lit, but other than that, my participation is limited to the occasional pop-in to take a photo and post it online so my mother sees that I haven't forgotten the Lord.

I was born in a lil ol' town called Terrell, Texas. I know you haven't heard of it because nobody has—unless you're Jamie Foxx. Then you *have* heard of it because you were born there too. Yes, Jamie Foxx and my mom went to school together. No, they didn't date. No, Jamie Foxx is not my dad. Yes, I wish he were. Just kidding, daddy-who-is-not-Jamie-Foxx-but-should've-been. (Isaac, you're cool. I love you. Thanks for contributing to my hot DNA.)

Terrell is a small town. Growing up, the two big restaurants you could go to were Dairy Queen and Sac-a-Burger. Our biggest claim to fame was that Bonnie and Clyde stayed in the local jail in the 1930s. I'm not even sure that that's true, but it was our small-town lore. I *loved* spending my formative years there.

A lot of my relatives lived on the same hill in Kemp, the town over, and we'd hop around from house to house whenever we pleased. My cousins and I were those wild, barefoot, country children, running the streets, picking fruits, stealing slices of pie from my Aunt Bettie Jean. No invitation needed; it was like our own little hippie commune except there weren't any white people in need of a haircut and a shave. Overall, it was really idyllic. It was. The further from home I get, the more I realize what a unique blessing it was to grow up with a lot of family around, especially when you have a family as incredible as mine.

Kemp is the kind of town where if you drive through it—and let's face it, you'd only be driving *through*—you'd practically raise the population by a whole percentage point. It's the kind of town where everybody knows your name, and I was related to all those everybodies. And like most teeny tiny communities, church was the centerpiece that held us all together, the core of our society. Our church was Won't He Do It Missionary Baptist Church.

I loved that place. It's exactly what you'd expect a Missionary Baptist church in a small Texas town of 1,200 people would be. It was right off Highway 175, down the street from the Dairy Queen, on the outskirts of town, and across the street from the cemetery where my family members were buried, are buried, and will be buried. (Except for me. I want a popping cemetery with movie premieres and hot people feeling each other up while picnicking on my grave. I'm looking at you, Hollywood Forever.)

To get to the church, you'd have to take Tolosa Road, turn left, away from the cemetery, and drive up the gravelly track that'd rock the car back and forth and jumble you around like a pack of cigarettes. The gravel dust would fly up around the car and settle on the top. It always smelled like earth and perfume, and it was all very country. If it isn't clear, *I love country.*

The church itself was a small brick building, but to me as a kid it seemed enormous. An institution. Even now, the whole place expands in my memory, taking up much more space than it should. The building was shotgun style: a room that led to a room, that led to a room, that led to THE ROOM, where everyone would congregate. That little church is where I saw my first true performance. And when I say *performance*, I mean *per-for-MANCE.* And the performer who gave that *per-for-MANCE* was Reverend Johnson.

Just like the church is larger than life in my head, so is Reverend Johnson. He was a tall man with large hands, and was very old . . . or maybe not? I was a kid, so he could've been in his forties and my kid brain just processed any age over twenty-five as old. Everyone in the country looks older than they are because country people don't care about Botox and they *don't* avoid the sun. They're too busy surviving life and enjoying nature to care what their skin is looking like. In Kemp, the men would dress like they were still living in the Civil Rights era, and Reverend Johnson was no different. He had all the MLK fits, which made him even more commanding up at the pulpit. Reverend Johnson is, to this day, one of the most prolific preachers that I've ever seen. I've been to church in Pittsburgh, New York, Los Angeles, Georgia, basically everywhere I've ever lived or worked, and I've never seen anyone even come close to Reverend Johnson. Dude could've been a televangelist and raked it all in if he wanted, but he chose to preach in Kemp. He chose *us*.

Reverend Johnson's sermons weren't just speeches: they were songs, they were dances, they were rhythm and movement that left your heart in your throat and your stomach at your knees. He'd preach so hard, he'd be sweating through his Jim Crow–era suits. Reverend Johnson's sermons were where I learned the power of putting on a show, of precisely telling stories, of choreographing your movements for an audience. The man would preach like he was a pop singer, luring us in with his voice, building the anticipation, and then dropping the beat. Damn, did Reverend Johnson know how to hit a climax. I was always struck by how powerful it must feel up there. If I weren't a performer, I'd be a pastor

4

for sure. It's all setups, breakdowns, and callbacks—the same as my comedy shit, just with biblical stakes. Reverend Johnson's style of performance really resonated with me. He would sing-yell, his voice bouncing off the wood-paneled walls and into the blood-brown carpet; it was electrifying. There were a lot of "AND THE LORDs" as well as a bunch of "HE WILLs."

Reverend Johnson made putting on a show seem like a noble thing to do as an adult. Not . . . you know, corny as fuck like starting a comedy career.

The thing I loved most about Reverend Johnson was that he was an honest man. He didn't hide his past; he led his congregation with humility. A lot of preachers rack their image up because they want to be seen as holy figures, perfect leaders, role models for the community. But we all know they are doing just as much sinning as we are. Take, for example, Brooklyn's Bishop of Bling, Lamor Whitehead.

GOD, GIVING, AND GUCCI

This is one of my favorite scams ever. Have you heard of the Bling Bishop of Brooklyn, the Pastor Gucci himself, Lamor Whitehead? I am obsessed with this ridiculous man. Lamor Whitehead was (is?) the head of a congregation no one's ever heard of called Leaders of Tomorrow International Ministries. Actually, Lamor founded Leaders of Tomorrow International Ministries shortly after he got out of prison for fraud. The man found God in Sing Sing, and the same week he got out, he decided to preach the Good Lord's word above a Haitian restaurant in southeast Brooklyn. Okay, Bishop, I'm here for it. We're all multidimensional! We're all sinners! You do you, Pastor Gucci!

The Bling Bishop was primarily known for his sick drip and for being close friends with the mayor of New York Eric Adams. This man was always head to toe in all the names—Dolce & Gabbana, Fendi, and Donna Karan—talking about how the meek shall inherit the earth. Anyone who saw that thousand-dollar tracksuit and those million-pound rings on each finger and *didn't* know right away that dude was lying in the name of the Lord has never been to a Black church. I've said it on my podcast, and I'll say it again here: if you have Jesus piece money, you should *not* be pastoring. This man. And the church didn't even look that good. It was giving, like, Courtyard Marriott, but Courtyard Marriott breakfast buffet *after* they rolled away the cart. Bagels, but no bagel toaster. Summertime sadness. Obviously, the church was struggling with its Build-It Fund (a real thing that churches have), and I'm betting all the money was going toward the Bling Bishop's *gator boots with the pimped-out Gucci suits.*

This man was basically a big, blingy piñata. And one day, that big, blingy piñata got robbed . . . in the middle of a service, during a livestream. In the video, you can see three masked and armed robbers snatch up all the jewelry off this man's damn body (reportedly a million dollars' worth). It's no wonder! Now, of course, I do not think he deserved to be robbed—but I do think wearing a modest house in the Valley's worth of jewelry on your person into the center of Canarsie,

Brooklyn, might be asking for it a little bit. Dude, I'd rob you in the checkout line at Trader Joe's if you have that kind of money with that little sense. Rocking Gucci suits and chains as thick as an elephant's tail is an interesting choice for a *pastor*. I'm as much of a label whore as the next dude, but a man of God? C'mon now. According to Whitehead, Leaders of Tomorrow International Ministries was a "church of wealth, not a church of poverty." Dude had his hustle baked into the mission! He was preaching the so-called Prosperity Gospel: "If you love God, God will get you a boat. Amen. Don't waste your time on your spirituality, focus on concrete things you can hold in your hands like money, diamonds, chains! It's what God wants. Amen." Y'all. You all. Yawl.

Well, the robbery raised a lot of questions about the Leaders of Tomorrow International Ministries. Questions like *why?* and *how?* Mostly *how?* With the added media attention, Lamor Whitehead's past started cropping up, and what did the nosey nellies of the world uncover? Bro owed hundreds of thousands of dollars to many different groups of people in his life. (Should've sold a ring or two!) He even owed more than $400,000 to the construction company that built his $1.64-million house in New Jersey and the credit union that financed his Mercedes-Benz and Range Rover. Hmmmmm. . . . So this guy was getting robbed while he was robbing. A real Robbing the Hood kind of guy.

The more journalists and content-hungry podcast hosts began to dig into this man's past, the more stories of identity fraud and malfeasance they found. Because of this, the NYPD shifted gears from the whole livestream robbery investigation and, instead, rolled up on Bishop Gucci. I love a gaslighting, lying king, but this man went too far with his con. Cooking the books, not paying his contractors, but worst of all: stealing donations from parishioners. Badman behavior. Even today, the dude is still free as fuck, suing anyone who points out why his actions are a problem—which is an uh-oh emoji for me!

Leading a church draws big personalities and even bigger egos. Belonging to a church draws vulnerable people looking for love, support, guidance, and community. To quote a biblical fave: "Beware of false prophets, which come to you in sheep's clothing, but inwardly they are ravening wolves." Anything that looks too rich, too shiny, too powerful, is most likely a false prophet—even the church and the leadership within.

SORRY MS. JOHNSON

A thing that I—and probably everyone who attended the small church in Kemp—loved instantly about Reverend Johnson was he told the truth. In telling the truth, he would often talk about something called "backsliding." Backsliding is basically when the "devil" gets a hold of you and makes you do a bunch of fun stuff. Reverend Johnson was very honest about his backsliding. He had no problem telling us all about his past life doing shady shit around town. All the stories would always end the same way: Reverend Johnson got saved and he stopped all his backsliding. I know this is a common tale, but it all felt very earnest with Reverend Johnson. I connected with his unapologetic vulnerability about his past. Who wouldn't love to forget all their wild choices . . . like BAM! I'm born again. If I could, I'd be born again on my rent, born again on my car payments . . . Student loans? Sallie Mae, I don't owe you shit, that was dead me, I'm born again!

Church in Kemp wasn't just a weekly event; it was everything. Church is where you'd go for love, life, death, and whatever else there is between love, life, and death. Wednesdays were for prayer meetings. Tuesdays were for choir rehearsal, and Sundays were, you guessed it, for church service. My whole family was at the church on Sundays. My grandfather was a deacon and very involved with leadership. I was in the choir with my cousins. My aunts and uncles went, and my parents did too. Church was your living room outside your living room.

My favorite part of church, aside from Reverend Johnson's performances, was choir. If you're lucky, you'll have a choir who can *sang*. And this choir could *s-a-n-g*. I loved performing with the choir. If I walk into church and see a kick drum, I'm just not going to stay for the music. Kick-drum church music is trash. For the God unsubscribers in the audience, kick-drum church music is the kind you'll see on late-night television, on those programs trying to get you to buy miracle spring water. White people—hands in the air, eyes closed? That's kick-drum church music. I'll stick to my sanging, thank you. "Take My Hand" by Shawn McDonald is a bop, though, so this isn't shade to *all* the white Christian music girlies.

Reverend Johnson's wife and first lady of the church, Ms. Pat, was the one who kept us busy with choir things. Ms. Pat was basically a celebrity around our country church parts—both of them were. Reverend Johnson and Ms. Pat were the Bey and Jay of Missionary Baptists in Kemp, Texas. Just as Reverend Johnson was the best real-life performer I'd ever seen, Ms. Pat was one of the most glamorous women I'd ever seen. I loved Ms. Pat. I used to watch her sitting in the First Lady of the Church spot in the first pew, her hair always neatly done, her church crown perfectly pinned in. Ms. Pat carried herself with such grace and composure, a real stunner of a human. She kept her boobs high and mighty for the Lord. Oh my gosh, yes, and her smile. She had a gorgeous smile. If Ms. Pat had ever moved to LA, she would've cleaned up. I don't know, maybe she was average? I tend to remember people hotter, especially when they're nice, and Ms. Pat was really nice. No, she must have been a hottie for the most high—I just know it. Anyway, I really loved spending my childhood in this little, dusty brick church in the middle of Nowhere, Texas. . . . Then everything went downhill.

The shift happened when I was fourteen years old, the year my cousin Valerie died in a horrible and unexpected way. Valerie was—I hate saying "was"—the glue that kept our big-spirited family together. I idolized her. I didn't have any older sisters, so when I snuck sleepovers in with my best friend/cousin Eric (her younger brother), I spied on her to learn what the cool girls did. Valerie was like a chic auntie who might offer you a sip of beer or steal your Alicia Keys CD. (Val, if you can read this, don't think I forgot!!!) Not only was Valerie gorgeous inside and out, but more important, she was sharp and *funny*. I loved her humor and loved even more how it made me feel like we were both always in on the same joke. Valerie knew what she wanted and would go after it and get it. She had so much promise, and it makes no sense that she was taken from us at such a young age.

Valerie was twenty-one years old. Valerie was a new mom with abs. Valerie had just been promoted to senior airman in the Air Force. On January 9, in 2006, Valerie was driving down to Mississippi to help with hurricane-relief efforts, and the car flipped. My family was devastated. We're still devastated. The unexpected tragedies, the ones that creep on you, are really a bitch. We found out like you do in the movies, where the service members come to your home on an afternoon when you least expect it, and quietly, promptly destroy the life you've known and hand you one you don't want—one without your cousin.

Because Valerie died while on active duty, the Air Force gave my family a sum of money. I don't know how much, but it was some. Southern and Missionary Baptists believe in the Lord, obviously, and so during this time, my family clung to that belief harder to try to make some sense of this senseless heartbreak. My uncle, a steadfast believer in the Lord even through unfathomable tragedy, tithed some of that sum to the church. And that's when everything changed.

As soon as that coin hit the basket, Reverend Johnson was like, "We NEED to build a new church!" Like? For real? For the Lord? There are like forty-six people here, and half of them are in their eighties. What the fuck are we going to build, Reverend? But of course, a little money shows up at the door, and the capitalist monster comes creeping right in, right through the pews.

Shortly after my uncle's heartfelt donation, Reverend Johnson had a new church show up on an eighteen-wheeler. Literally just Amazon Prime'd a new church to the door. Did you know you could do that? Dude SkyMalled that bitch into our hood as if that's something a town no bigger than my college dorm needed: a larger, shinier church. The new church was big and made of metal—a tin can church. There was no warmth, no history to the metal walls, no soul. There was no longer a crunchy gravel parking lot where dust swirled 'round your car until it settled on the roof. Just flat asphalt. It wasn't the little brick church across the street where my grandma was laid to rest anymore. It was . . . something different. The bolder, colder church I could've lived with, could've gotten used to, but then Reverend Johnson started to change, too.

Black churches are more about community than about religion. Black church is about making friends. Gossiping, laughing, fucking, judging, dating, loving . . . shopping— all of it. At my church, there was a group of little old ladies who would save up their money for church-sponsored excursions, and one of those excursions was a trip to Dallas, where they'd go shopping at JCPenney. I'm going to sound bougie, but I wish I could fuck with a JCPenney the way these little old church ladies did. They treated the place like it was Dior on Rodeo Drive. It was the highlight of their year! My life would be *so* much better if I spent my days dreaming of yearly trips to JCPenney, bursting with joy at the thought of all the moderately priced garments hanging under those bright fluorescent lights! Instead, I live in a city full of empty people who will never be satiated with all they have. I don't know what's wrong with me, why I can't be satisfied and enthralled with a good ol' southern JCPenney. I'll figure it out in therapy . . .

So these little old ladies were getting ready for their big trip, and I remember sitting in the sermon and Reverend Johnson decides he wants to talk about "pride and greed." Like, okay, you playin' the hits. But then his focus shifts to these little old JCPenney church ladies. He was like, "The ladies going to Dallas? That's money we should put into the church. That's money we should give to the LORDDDDDD!" A big *hmmmmmm* from me. Because bro's singing "AND THE LORDs" and "HE WILLs," but the feeling had shifted. Like I said, Reverend Johnson was a pop singer, and church is a pop song: if the beat is good, we don't give a fuck what you're saying. But that's where the shakedown happens. People get caught up in the beat without listening to what's behind the lyrics. Reverend Johnson still had the beats, but my blossoming little scammer ear started to pick up on something deeper. I was like, "Wait a second, these lyrics suck. Let the JCPenney gals have their fun." Like, Reverend, didn't you just roll up to

SCAM LIFE LESSON

Beware of the beat, listen to the lyrics.

the joint with a big, fancy tin can church that no one wanted or needed? **Beware of the beat, listen to the lyrics.**

This is around the same time when a woman named Leena entered the picture. In church terms, we'd call Leena . . . *a hussy.* I didn't make that up and I'm not condoning it; that's just what women like Leena were called. As the church got shinier and richer with my family's tragedy-money, Leena started moving closer and closer to the front pew until one day she sat right down next to Ms. Pat. And well, you know how I said church was a place of worship and gossip? Well, the worship whisperers were claiming that *Reverend Johnson was fucking Leena.* *shaking my damn head* This man, y'all, he was backsliding real hard.

One day, I'll never forget, during one of Reverend Johnson's more intense performances, with a lot of HE-WILLing about, Leena was sitting in the First Lady pew also feeling the spirit—the hussy spirit—when all of a sudden she started feverishly fanning herself while making eyes with Reverend Johnson. They thought they were being sneaky, but we all knew what was going on.

Oh, before I forget, our little country church had a funeral-home sponsor. (This will all come together, I promise.) It was like those gas stations that also have a car wash because we have to be efficient out in the middle of nowhere. And on hot Texas summer days, the funeral home would give out these fans: a hard piece of paper on a popsicle stick with the name of the funeral home on one side and a picture of Martin Luther King on the other.

So Reverend Johnson is building up to the climax of the sermon, and he's getting louder, singing more, getting frantic, and secretly-but-not-really-so-secretly flirting with Leena. It was so clear to the whole church that they were fucking. They're tossing eyes at each other, being so blatant. Messy. As Reverend Johnson gets closer to the climax, Leena starts fanning herself harder. Then, Reverend Johnson hits the high note, and Leena's fan drifts from her chest, to her stomach, and then she starts fanning . . . between . . . her legs. RIGHT UP THE SKIRT! MLK fully aerating her coochie. Really in the ho spirit. I was a kid, and even I was like, WHAT THE FUCK IS HAPPENING?!?!?!? I can't emphasize how small the town is—you could've fit all of us on twenty Greyhound buses. . . . Like, Rev. and Leena, girl, where y'all fucking?! How do you even find a place to go? What in the hell?!

Remember when I told you my grandpa was a deacon? Well, part of his deacon duties was staying after church, putting on the white gloves, and counting the tithings. One thing you should know about my grandpa is he was really a stand-up guy, an important member of the community, one of the most moral men out there. He even has a local holiday named after him as a thank-you for all the service he did on the Kemp City Council. A real one, my gramps. One day, around this same time, my grandfather begins to realize that the books weren't booking and the math wasn't mathing. Reverend Johnson had gone from backsliding to backslided: he was stealing money from the church, flush from my family's tragedy. Shortly after my grandfather came to this conclusion, Reverend Johnson was removed from the church, and we never saw him again. Ever.

Such a shame. Reverend Johnson really was an amazing performer. He made me excited about church and made my dreams feel like a possibility. But it just goes to show that even the most talented of us, the most connected to God, struggle to **fight the lure of shiny, pretty things**. Reverend Johnson made me excited about the art of performing as a kid, but he also taught me not to trust religion too deeply— not to subscribe to one way of believing, one way of doing things, because if you do, you're bound to get disappointed.

SCAM LIFE LESSON

Fight the lure of shiny, pretty things.

To me, religion is a casino, and I don't want to go all in on one hand. I'm betting on everything. I put some money on Jesus. Allah. Gimme Buddhism too. I just need to believe—hope for—something more. At the end of the day, I really do hope we don't disappear to where we were before we were alive. It sucked. It was dark; I couldn't form thoughts or memories. I couldn't feel joy or sadness. Nah, I don't really want to go back there. I'd rather believe there's something else, something after . . . anything. But still, I don't believe in the scam of the church. To each her own. My connection to God comes from nature and other hippie-dippie shit. Like I said, I'll bet a little on everything. But the spirituality of fresh air and good vibes is where it's at for me.

The scam of religion is that it makes people live in absolutes: right vs. wrong, good vs. bad, life vs. death, abundance vs. lack, God vs. devil. People who want to do things right, to live a good life of abundance and God, are going to gravitate toward anything that promises a clear-cut solution— whether that's a church or a weight-loss commercial—but it's important to know nothing is entirely good or bad, right or wrong. Everything is everything. When people are handed two options and told to pick one, they spend their whole lives justifying their choice—even when it doesn't feel right. But life's not like that: it's not binary. There are never only two options. It's more textured. The sooner we learn how to coexist with the complication, the sooner we can accept ourselves and feel satiated with what we have . . . just like those JCPenney ladies. Amen.

Job Scams

Did I ever think I'd be searching for little baggies of cocaine in the lush, green fields of the Hamptons while Paul McCartney waited for me to bring him his off-menu eggplant? No. But that's exactly what I found myself doing the summer of 2015. It was the summer before I was going to finally move to Hollywood to pursue acting for real = for real, precisely as I'd been planning since kindergarten. But in order to move to Hollywood, I needed money—lots of it. So I took a job with Moby's, a pop-up, summer-only, farm-to-table restaurant with enough hyphens in the description to draw a moneyed crowd. Name someone famous and I've probably refilled their sparkling-water glass. I'm not kidding: Robert Downey Jr., Bono, Jon Bon Jovi, Fat Joe, and more—I quenched all them bitches' thirst.

I understood the importance of money from a young age. It started with those scammy-ass Scholastic Book

Fairs. You know the ones? With those shiny markers, smelly pencils, and hard erasers that don't erase shit. That was my—and I'm guessing many of y'all's—first introduction to capitalism. Because you had to have *cash on hand* to be able to go to those things and buy something. It's jarring! At my school, if you didn't have the money to buy something, you had to stay in the classroom with the other poors, doing your boring-ass worksheets. No Clifford or Junie B. Jones to distract you from your sad, lower-class life. How dare those Scholastic motherfuckers shame little kids for not having money.

The catalogs? Oh my God, remember those? Why are we paying taxes into the public school system, into our community parks, while kids were still out there, in the street, going door-to-door selling wrapping paper? How is it even a sustainable industry? Pimping random junk out to your parents' coworkers so you can win a Razor scooter for ten times what it's worth. I tried doing one of those catalog sales *once* and hated everything about it. Sure, I sold a bunch of stuff—I'm a scammer—but my mom and I ended up moving before it all came for distribution so I unintentionally ripped off my whole neighborhood. Like I said before, little kids *should not* have to work a job—even if that "job" is fundraising by selling enormous buckets of stale-ass popcorn. Little kids shouldn't need to figure out how to find the money to pay for something that should be free—like food, books, and writing utensils. Yet we've normalized this practice. We've accepted this bullshit for years and years.

Recently, I saw a quote floating around the internet that said, "Tradition is just peer pressure from the dead." Well, I'm not about to get peer pressured by any dead people, thank you. Running a scam not on my own terms felt gross to me, so after the whole catalog fundraiser fiasco, I never sold anything again. If I was going to buy into the scam of capitalism, I was going to do it for myself, not make a big corporation richer off my hard work. I was going to get my money, too.

Jobs—99 percent of us need 'em; 99 percent of us don't want 'em. But they're our meal ticket . . . literally (and I'm using the OG version of *literally*, like when it used to mean what it actually means). Because I learned at a young age that I never wanted to be limited by how much money I have, I've had a lot of jobs. So many employments. I'm the minimum wage Keke Palmer. I was a tour guide in college, or a Pathfinder as they were called at the University of Pittsburgh. That job was dope because I was able to test out material for my future comedy sets on prospective students and their parents. Then there was the time I was a sushi hoochie, selling very expensive sushi at a place called Roku while wearing a tiny denim dress that got tinier with each wash. I also used to work for Balfour rings, where my only job requirement was to make enormous, 1980s-era class rings sexy again. (I threw a Facebook page up and called it a day.)

Listen, the American Job Market is a scam. Most gigs are a roll of the dice. Sometimes you luck into one where you get paid to talk into a microphone while hanging out with your friends; other times you're dodging bullets while wearing booty shorts and trying to sell some tequila. I've done both. All in all, I've learned that if a job seems too good to be true, then it probably is. Which brings me to the Silicon Valley Theft Bro.

THE SILICON VALLEY THEFT BRO

Kyle Sandler is not the type of person you'd notice in a crowd. He's a lil' shorty with a baby face and a sweet smile. When I look at this dude, I get strong Magic-the-Gathering-close-the-door-Mom realness. Despite his youthful drip, Kyle was a moneyed man who struck it big on the West Coast as a Google executive. And like all Google executives who make a ton of money off harassing millennials with Better Help ads, Kyle decided to give back to "the community." Hm. Just any old community? Okay, Kyle, what you got cooking?

In October 2014, while most people in charitable moods were dumping buckets of ice on their damn heads, Kyle moved to Opelika, Alabama, and opened a tech startup incubator called Round House. Oh, so when you say "help the community," you mean "help the tech-bro community." Got it.

The residents of the small East Alabama town took note of Kyle's flashy car and fast-paced attitude and, little by little, started to invest in his "tech startup incubator." As buzz and investments grew for Round House, Kyle began attracting bigger fish, like John McAfee, a wizard-genie-warlock who founded McAfee computer security company. All you need to know about John McAfee is that he was an eccentric antivirus mogul who once promised to "eat his own dick" if Bitcoin didn't hit $1 million by 2020. (For those wondering, Bitcoin did not hit $1 million by 2020, but John never got around to the whole dick-eating thing before he passed in 2021.) Definitely a man you'd want backing your business!

Once McAfee was on board, the city of Opelika was too, and a number of small businesses started working out of Round House, including a business thought up by thirteen-year-old Taylor Rosenthal, a boy with sandy blond hair, freckles, and no business running a startup. I guess, what's a serial tech entrepreneur but a thirteen-year-old boy trapped in a man's body? Taylor's idea was basically to create a vending machine that pops out first-aid gear to those who need it: cut-up athletes, kids with scraped knees, drunk Coachella babes. I have to give it to him, this kid's idea was not half bad . . . America's health care system is ass.

I'm not the only one who thought Taylor's idea was a decent one—so did Kyle! Out of the goodness of his golden heart—and for a 30 percent stake in Taylor's company—Kyle registered to be "the agent" of RecMed LLC. Shortly after, *Inc. Magazine* named Taylor one of twenty teen entrepreneurs "set for success." This article generated so much attention around Taylor's business that some *mystery* investors offered him a *$30 million* buyout.

I know for sure if I got offered $30 million, you'd never see me again. I'd disappear before I'd get murdered or lose it all.

This is probably the craziest part of this whole saga because Taylor turned down the money. He was like, "Thirty million? Nah, I'm good. I still have my bar mitzvah coin." Know your worth, Taylor. Know your worth. Taylor later said he was holding out for a $50 million buyout, and Kyle told CNBC that they were "in talks with a 'major consumer product company in the home and health-care space.'" Taylor's family claims that Kyle even showed them paperwork from the "major consumer product company in the home and health-care space," rumored to be Johnson & Johnson. This dude really said he had *both* Johnsons interested.

However, three months later, things took an abrupt turn: Round House closed its doors for good, and Kyle Sandler was a wanted man. After his eventual arrest, Kyle told the media that his tech startup incubator had simply run out of money. That's nearly $2 million. Where did all your idea money go, Kyle? I mean, we all knew he was going to play Opelika like this, right? Shortly after Round House closed down, the truth began to come out. In addition to never being a rich Google CEO, Kyle was actually a criminal—convicted in Maryland and North Carolina for attempted theft and forgery. Even though he had been convicted, he never served any prison time. Cute. We love a conviction and no prison time. Just like . . . you opted out of jail, Kyle? I didn't know you could go to court, get a guilty sentence, and be like, "Alright bet. Thank y'all so much. Have a nice day. See ya later!"

On top of having a checkered criminal past and zero money, Kyle had also lied to Taylor's family about the $30 million deal. Straight up made the whole thing up, knowing the kind of too-cool-for-school hype around Taylor it'd cause. Oh, and that Johnson & Johnson paperwork? Fake. A damn shame, I would've liked to get my meds by pressing P43 on a vending machine.

Well folks, this continues to prove that the tech world is especially fertile grounds for cons, frauds, and straight-up theft. Americans put a lot of value on what we *do*. Because of this, when there's, let's say, a recession, people become vulnerable to schemers, especially when those schemers allude to money, stability, and bringing value back to your identity. Even though I respect his hustle and there are no ethical choices under capitalism, don't let yourself get swindled by the Kyle Sandlers of the world. **Put value on who you are, not what you do.** That way, when it comes to finding a job or selling an idea, you'll be able to think with a clear mind and protect yourself from getting conned.

I learned this lesson early on in my career . . . Let me take you back to the summer of 2011 when young Laci was a sophomore at the University of Pittsburgh.

SCAM LIFE LESSON

Put value on who you are, not what you do.

THE DRUG FRONT DIVA OF DIVES

Honestly? Probably the least capitalistic job I've ever had was working for a drug front in Pittsburgh. I didn't set out to work at a drug front, obviously, but it was one of my first real non-catalog-selling adult jobs and I loved every minute of it.

All my friends decided they were going to spend the summer after freshman year club-hopping in Cabo, and I'm not going to lie, that sounded like a pretty fucking fantastic way to spend my final summer as a teenager. But I knew that the second I graduated school, I was going to move to New York and finally become an actor—which meant I'd be poor for a long time, possibly forever, which costs a bitch a lot of money. It's expensive to be poor! So I needed to figure out how to make cash fast *and* how to hide it from the government. So instead of going to Cabo, I signed up for a bartending course at Elite Bartending School Pittsburgh's #1 Bartending School (possibly Pittsburgh's only bartending school, so hey, they didn't lie!).

My first day of class was a trip. I arrived at Elite Bartending School Pittsburgh's #1 Bartending School, located on the second floor of Dormont Village, a boring-looking strip mall with a Payless and Great Clips. (Yes, what you're picturing is exactly accurate.) I got upstairs, walked through the door, and was surprised to see a fake bar setup. Everything = fake. The bottles were filled with food-dyed water; the "glass" cups were plastic. Truly the first "set" I'd ever been on. Nothing was as it seemed. I was fascinated.

Very quickly, I found out that bartending school is an excellent place to learn how to count to four, slice citrus, and avoid what my #1 instructor called a "herpe hold"— aka holding cocktail glasses from the top where people's mouths touch. It didn't exactly require high-level thinking. Although I was pretty sure no one would actually order a Singapore Sling, a Cuba Libre, or an Adios Motherfucker, I did learn how to make all three *and* hand pour three bottles at once . . . a skill I did end up using on an episode of *iCarly*, so money well spent, I guess.

After $600 and forty hours, I was a proud graduate of Elite Bartending School Pittsburgh's #1 Bartending School—they even gave me an official diploma (a paper certificate they printed out in front of us). Nearly immediately, I hit the Strip District, a little part of Pittsburgh hugging the Allegheny River where all the best bars were, with my résumé and official diploma. A week of unsuccessful applications in, I began to realize I maybe had some factors working against me: For one, the Elite Bartending School certificate didn't do shit. People were like, "Bitch, you have zero experience. Bye." For two, I realized that all the bars I was applying to didn't have any Black bartenders. My odds of getting employment were not looking good. It was time to pivot. Yet another important lesson in the scam life: **know when to pivot**.

SCAM LIFE LESSON
Know when to pivot.

If everyone is too dumb to see my greatness, I thought, *I'm going to have to show them.* Door knocking wasn't working, so I turned to my closest business adviser: Craigslist.com. When you're struggling, the Craigslist Gigs section is always there to pick you up. Pretty instantly, I stumbled upon the most Craigslist job posting that ever was: "Models Wanted." I clicked because I have a banging body and a pretty face, and I was delighted to see the job requirements were basically "promote Summer Jam while looking cute and being charming." All things I could do. At the bottom of the posting, I saw that they were holding auditions that week. *Auditions?* Already, this was speaking my love language way more than bartending ever did. I immediately began digging through my dresser, looking for the tightest, smallest clothing I could find. I found a horrible headshot from the time when I begged my mom to gift me headshots for my high school graduation, thinking that Mr. Hollywood was going to welcome me into a life of fame and celebrity the second I became of age. I briefly considered bringing it before deciding this wasn't a headshot type of affair.

The morning of the audition, I flat ironed my hair, painted on a bright-pink lip, and wiggled into some short-shorts from rue21 and an American Apparel crop top. To complete the lewk, I added seven-inch platform Jessica Simpson heels made of vegan leather, aka *plastique*.

The audition was held at a place called the Bar & Lounge, and when I got to the small, brick storefront, I was kind of confused because it just looked like a seedy dive bar. Not a place you'd hold auditions for models/promo girls. There was a sandwich board out front advertising $2 Miller Lites and a semiabandoned building next door. But before I could change my mind, a couple of other hot girls walked in and I knew I was in the right place.

Inside, the bar was a lot longer and dirtier than it looked on the outside. There were a few $2 Miller Lite–looking dudes watching the girls come in, all of whom immediately went up the shiny black stairs. I popped my shoulders back, put my chin up, and followed suit. Upstairs, it was immediately clear that Shayla, the head promo girl, would be holding the auditions. Behind her was The Boss, a short Black dude who seemed very influential solely based on the way he carried himself. He was one of those guys you take a look at and are like, *I wouldn't be surprised if he's done murders.* He had a quiet kind of importance that scared me a little bit.

Once all the girls had filed up the stairs, the interview process began, but there weren't the traditional interview questions like: "What's your greatest weakness?" It was more like, "Do you have Friday and Saturday nights free?" So Shayla does my interview, and I put on my biggest, most magnetic smile and tell her that "Yes, I have Friday and Saturday nights free." I'm thrilled to report that I aced the interview and got the job. Before I left, Shayla gave me a shirt that was a couple sizes smaller than it should've been and an address for where I needed to be *that* Friday. My first real job.

I wish I could remember the club where the rest of this story takes place, but here's the scam about clubs: they always want to be the hottest, newest thing on the block, so they're always changing their names. It's been happening for decades. First, it's the Greystone Manor Supper Club, and then they close down, move the bar to a different poorly lit corner, and now it's the Nightingale Plaza.

During college, my friends and I used to hit up Dreams Nightclub because ladies got in free before 11 p.m. and they had "free" transportation from campus—which just turned out to be off-duty school buses. Sexy! Then the club got stale . . . so we cooled on it. One day, a friend of mine showed up with a new flyer advertising Club 21. It had good drink specials, fresh vibes, so we were like, "Okay, let's give Club 21 a try." We walked in, looked around, and realized it's just fucking Dreams again! They painted the outside, moved the bar to the other side of the room, and changed the sign out front. By junior year, we were getting hip to the scam. A few times, my friends came with new flyers and I pointed out that the address was always the same. "It's just Dreams, you guys." Then, one day, everyone was talking about the Mosaic Lounge: it was cool; it was new; it was the place to be on a Friday night. I told my friends, "No, it's Dreams. I'm not gonna get got again." But then they showed me the address on the flyer, and sure enough, it was different. So I was like, "Fuck it, let's go." We showed up to the building, which was suspiciously close to Dreams, and once we walked in, I immediately realized *it was just the back entrance into Dreams.* They fucking got us. That's club culture for you— no originality, no creativity, just expensive alcohol with no mixers and the nastiest cocktails you'll ever find.

Alllll of that is to say, I do not remember the club where my first day as a promo girl was, but it's exactly like every club on the planet: ass. Shayla and a few of the girls arrived shortly after I did, and I began to mirror what they were doing, which was not much. In fact, most of the job seemed to be trailing The Boss around, making him look important. It was so dark that no one could even see our itty-bitty baby Summer Jam promo shirts. I honestly don't know how this was advertising anything other than our titties.

At a certain point, The Boss walked upstairs where there were two rooms separated by a short hallway. We dutifully followed him up and lingered between the two rooms. I was finding the job to be pretty boring at that point, but a job's a job. Then, the vibe changed in an instant. Someone came up the stairs, and I looked over in time to see him pull out a shiny, metallic object and turn it sideways. (This was when the culture was all about turning your gun sideways when you shoot.) Before I could say or think "Oh shit!" flashes came from the barrel of the gun and I saw someone fall. Someone else yelled, "THEY'RE TRYING TO KILL THAT GUY!" and the whole club started running. I'm a person who likes to go with the flow so I was like, "Okay. We are running now. Cool. Gotta get my cardio in anyway." I do have to shout out my girl Jessica Simpson: those sturdy-ass heels saved my life.

As we started down the stairs toward the exit, the cops burst in and immediately began spraying mace like it was air freshener. Everyone started gagging except The Boss, who was wheezing his little short-king crown off. I immediately recognized that signature asthmatic wheeze because I have the same one. Shayla took one look at The Boss through her swollen, teary eyes and began shrieking, *"GET HIS INHALER! GET HIS INHALER!"* It was by far one of the goofiest scenes I've ever been a part of—and I've done improv for yearssss. The Boss seemed a lot less scary hands on knees, butt sticking out.

After we pulled ourselves from the rubble, the other promo girls rolled their eyes, sucked their teeth, and wobbled off in their platform heels—only mildly annoyed by the whole shooting thing. Like straight up, they were completely unfazed by the bullets flying around our heads. I will say, this shooting felt safer because it was Black people shooting. When Black people shoot, there's usually a hit. No bullets wasted on bystanders. It's not like the random angry basement white boy shootings plaguing America where they are just shooting anybody. Actually, I guess all races can shoot indiscriminately . . . maybe this was just a lie I told myself to feel like I wasn't in a shooting. Damn, I guess I was in a shooting. I'll talk to my therapist about this, too . . .

After somehow making it safely home that night, I decided being a promo girl was not for me. I did not want to die in a corny club, wearing a toddler's t-shirt. If I'm going out, it had better be epic and not . . . trashy. The next day,

I took the bus back to the Bar & Lounge with my Summer Jam t-shirt neatly folded in my lap. Even though The Boss probably didn't care about the shirt or about me, I have proper etiquette and knew I should quit in person— and return the shirt. I went back past the $2 Miller Lite sandwich board, past the same men at the counter, and upstairs where The Boss was preparing for another round of auditions. "Thank you for the opportunity, but this isn't for me," I quickly told him, handing him the shirt. He looked me up and down and smiled. "You know," he said, "I have other things you can do. Do you want to work here? Bartend? I saw that on your résumé." (I didn't bring my seventeen-year-old headshot to the audition, but I did bring a résumé just in case.) I said yes before he even finished his sentence. Finally, my Elite Bartending School Pittsburgh's #1 Bartending School degree was going to pay off! All it took was some booty-shorts, a little club shooting, and quitting my job to get a job.

I started the next day—no paperwork, no intake, no onboarding. Just good ol' under-the-table fun!

When I got to the Bar & Lounge for Take #2 of my summer college employment, I walked through the doors right as the chorus to "Somebody That I Used to Know" hit. I remember what song was playing because the Bar & Lounge played the radio—commercials and all—and that song was on every day, sixteen times a day, all summer long. It was like *Groundhog Day*: "You didn't have to cuuuuut me off!" An hour later, "You didn't have to cuuuuut me off!" By the end of my time at the Bar & Lounge, Gotye must've been cut off like 6,000 times. That song still haunts my brain to this day. Another one to explore with my therapist . . .

I lingered near the door until The Boss came out to greet me. He introduced me to the one other bartender, a light-skinned Black girl chopping limes with purple hair and a scowl on her face, and promptly disappeared. The girl behind the bar was Mixie. (Probably still is.) Yes, a bartender named Mixie. Mixie was a bit older than me, with a pretty face and a sloppy-sexy fit: low-cut, tight tank tops, with fraying straps. I could tell she did not want to be my friend, which was fine. I like a challenge. I gave her my biggest, brightest cheerleader smile and a "Hi." She handed me a bar rag. Okay, so it was going to take some time to ingratiate myself with Mixie—not a problem.

Mixie was (and remains) one of the few people who could resist my charm. I tried to make jokes with her or talk about regulars, but she was completely uninterested in speaking with me. She would just show me how to do things without much chitchat. And the way Mixie did things was very different from what I had learned at Elite Bartending School Pittsburgh's #1 Bartending School. For starters, she'd scoop ice with a *glass*—anyone who has ever worked in the service industry knows to n-e-v-e-r use a glass. If that thing shatters in the ice bucket, you have to burn the whole place down. I gently tried to suggest we use a plastic cup, but Mixie wasn't having it: "This is how we do it here." That was basically the Bar & Lounge slogan. She showed me how to cut limes into the tiniest pieces you ever saw, because that was cheaper. She taught me how to pour beer: "Just put the glass down and pull the tap." When I suggested tilting the glass to avoid the foam, she just looked at me and said, "This is how we do it here." At the end of my shift, I was instructed to split my tips and take $42 out of the register. No paperwork or nada. I knew it wasn't normal, but what is? Besides, I find normal to be very boring.

My favorite part of the gig was the clientele. When I say this place was a dive, I mean it. There were a handful of regulars who'd come in day to day, most of them toothless, but the loveliest people I've ever worked for. We had that $2 Miller Lite special and attracted $2 Miller Lite kind of people. One day, a pretty, shiny woman came in for a $2 beer and began to chat me up. "You know, you're very pretty," she said.

I'd been used to this kind of flirtation from the clientele and was even more excited that it was a woman this time. "Thank you," I told her.

She continued, "I work across the street, you'd be great there."

"Oh, really? What do you do?" My interest was piqued. I wasn't making a lot of money at the Bar & Lounge, so maybe I could do both.

"It's the easiest job in the world," she said, casually sipping on her $2 beer. "All you need to do is rub a little oil on your titties and that's basically it." *Then* I understood what she did, remembering what kind of business was across the street.

I politely declined because sex work is *not* the easiest job in the world. Strippers are in shape. I work out, but I'm not in stripper shape. Sex workers workkkkk. I'm a big fan of what y'all do. I also think it's completely unfair that it's a profession that's looked down upon. You know if men had a pussy, it'd be on the stock market, but they're telling us we can't sell it? Hm. But regardless, I knew I was better cut out for the Bar & Lounge.

In general, the people who came into the bar were always very sweet. They didn't have a lot of money, and because our price point was really low, they didn't need it. Getting a tip at that bar meant a lot because I knew it meant a lot to the people who left it. The financial situation was the most curious thing—the place did not make a lot of money each day, half the people coming in were treating the register like their personal ATM, and yet it stayed open day in and day out.

The longer I worked at the Bar & Lounge, the more strange things began happening. One time, a young dude came in and asked for $50 out of the register. "It's cool," he told me. "I'm The Boss's son." Sus. "I don't think that's how business works," I told him, planting my feet at the register. I was halfway through my business degree at the Pitt and it wasn't like *I* knew how business worked either, but this just seemed shady.

Mixie pushed me aside and popped open the register. "Just give him the money, it's cool." She handed over the note, and the guy was gone. But I couldn't let it go. "We need a system, some kind of accounting," I told her as she went back to sloppily pouring a beer for a customer. "This is how we do it here," she responded with a shrug. I sighed and decided that I would create a system. So I began leaving little notes in the register: "Son took $50." "Baby Mama took $100." "Laci took $42." "Other son took $80." The next time I saw The Boss, I told him, "Hey, just so you know, I left some notes to help you keep track of where the money's going." He just laughed and said, "Laci, you really are smart. Look at you, college girl, writing notes." Pretty quickly I started putting two and five and nine together and was like, *Ohhhh, this is a front. Y'all ain't making money here. Okay, cool!*

Toward the end of summer, my friends already back from Cabo, I found out that a spot down the street from the Bar & Lounge was hiring bartenders at their very swanky bar called fl.2, which stood for Floor 2 (very original). Even though school was starting up again and my parents didn't want me working during schooltime, I still applied because I knew one day's pay at this cool hotel bar would probably add up to a week's worth of tips at the Bar & Lounge. The money was just too good to pass up.

SCAM LIFE LESSON

Always lie on your résumé.

This time, I was smart: I'd learned the hustle of lying on your résumé. (**Always lie on your résumé.** Just choose lies that are hard to fact-check and make sure you have the skills to back up what you write.) Instead of showing up with my bartending school certificate in my hands and a few months opening $2 Miller Lites under my belt, I showed up with a very phat résumé featuring a carefully embellished list of alllll the skills I'd learned as a "dedicated and passionate bartender for the Bar & Lounge." . . . I got the job. I promised to work only on weekends, so my parents let me keep it.

As the five-star hotel bar at the Fairmont Hotel in the middle of Downtown Pittsburgh, fl.2 was as opposite of the Bar & Lounge as you could get. The brass details, velvet chairs, and art-deco-meets-industrial vibe screamed money. There were zero sandwich boards and no $2 Miller Lite specials to be seen. They kept their expensive liquor hanging over our heads in a weird, glass sculptural shelf, like some sort of prize or warning. On my first day, I immediately learned that everything Mixie had taught me was wrong. Her freehand pour counts were off, dicing limes was never how you're supposed to cut them—even her Long Island Iced Teas were all wrong. Yet still, I found myself missing working with her. The Fairmont seemed to be all about appearances. No substance. No character. It was not my vibe at all. If I came in a few minutes late, you'd best believe there'd be a manager breathing down my neck talking about responsibility and accountability and all sorts of -ilities.

Watching rich couples sitting at the bar, staring at their phones, not saying a peep to each other, made me miss my old job and my old job people even more. I preferred the $2 Miller Lite folks over the five-star richies. The richies did give me Christmas bonus tips, and while the money was insane, the front had freedom and kindness that lingered with me.

A few months into the job, I came in to my scheduled shift only to find that there was already a bartender working behind the bar. Well, *that* was fast. My manager walked me to the back office and in a very cold, sterile, by-the-book type of way gave me the boot. I had rolled up late too many times (three times—which, fine). An automatic firing. I'd never been fired before, and my ego took a hit. Sure, I'm loud and wacky, but I'm also a perfectionist. My only weakness is being perpetually seven minutes late to everything—including that bougie booze job! I was an ADHD college student who would go on to have several jobs at once. *I do a lot of stuff.*

In fact, I've only been fired from a job one other time in all the years since then, and it was what led to my break in the entertainment industry. I was working at a privately owned restaurant in Beverly Hills when the dessert chef didn't show up. One of my tables had ordered a crème brûlée to celebrate a birthday. This was not a restaurant where you say no to the guests, so there I was in the back setting fire to some custard like I knew what I was doing. When I came out to serve the dessert, I saw that some very old rich fashion people had been seated in my section. In fashion, youth is currency, so when you're old, the only currency you have is power. By the looks on their faces, I could tell they were already pissed and ready to throw some power around. I arrived with my charm set to 11 and a complimentary bottle of wine . . . but it was over.

Nothing I could do would make them feel better about the fact that I hadn't greeted their table immediately because I was too busy trying not to burn down the entire kitchen. After they ate their meal and left, the rich lady wrote a letter to the restaurant about my bad behavior—which, can I remind you, was arriving at the table *five minutes after* they sat down BECAUSE I WAS FLAMBÉING. The restaurant was able to fire me on a technicality. (I hadn't reported the wine I'd comped for the table to make up for it—shoulda put a note in the register.) Luckily, my manager was cool and filled out the paperwork in a way that allowed me to get a fat unemployment check—mostly thanks to my pay at the sushi hoochie job. I took that government money and used it to pay my rent and bills so I could perform full-time. And that eventually led me to my first acting job for CollegeHumor and then a series regular role in—well, you'll see. I haven't been back to the service industry since. Thank you, shriveled-up fashion ghouls!

Both firings made me feel like I was just a number to my employer, like all the good work I'd done could be wiped out by a single small mistake (or three). That's exactly why the drug front, while still a job, was the least capitalistic one I've ever had. They didn't care about earning money; they cared about earning loyalty. And I fuck with that. Since the Bar & Lounge, I've had a lot of experience working weird jobs for shady people, and I love it. The shadier the establishment, the more fun the environment. At the Bar & Lounge, The Boss actually cared about my safety and satisfaction—people over profits and shit. He complimented me. He saw my potential and never looked at me like another cog in the machine—probably because if you're going to run a highly illegal business, you have to make sure your staff are taken care of.

Juxtaposing the jobs made me realize that I much prefer gritty hustlers to polished professionals. There was no energy, no personality at the hotel bar. We all have to hustle to make money, because money leads to resources, and resources lead to opportunities, and opportunities lead to freedom. We all just want freedom. But there's always got to be a way to make it fun. When you're out there making money, make sure The Man isn't scamming you; make sure you're scamming The Man.

Housing Scams

The second I graduated from college, I gathered up all my bartending money and moved to that big, sleepless bitch they call New York. I'd finally finished performing in my role of good student and could now become a student of good performance. Where better to dive into all that than New York City, babyyyy?! I dove straight into New York and, well, hit the bottom of the pool pretty quickly.

People say that you need two years in New York City to tell whether or not you're a New Yorker. I am here to report that I am not a New Yorker. New York puts me on edge, fam. I really couldn't stomach another day, sitting on the train, underground like a rat *with the rats*. I used to keep a corkscrew I stole from work in my hands as a weapon, like I was in some sort of service industry–themed production of *West Side Story*. On my walks home, I'd put that corkscrew between my middle and ring fingers, ready to . . . open-a-bottle-of-wine someone to death? The second I had to donkey-kick a creep down some subway stairs, I knew it was time to make my big move to Los Angeles. At the end of 2015, I had my pocket full of Paul McCartney tips and Los Angeles on the horizon.

Moving across the country is always tricky, especially when you don't know shit about the city you're moving to. All I *really* knew about Los Angeles was that if you wanted to, you could buy a $16 juice and drink it while watching Michael B. Jordan getting his iPhone fixed at the Grove.

When it came time for the dreaded "Look for Housing in an Expensive City on a Broke Girl Budget" thing, I decided to reach out to some friends who had already made the move to the West Coast to get some intel. The first person I contacted was my friend Angel. Angel and I were childhood friends from Frisco, Texas, where I spent my formative years after my mom and I moved out of Terrell for greener, more suburban-y pastures. Here's the thing about Frisco: it's white, y'all. Like *very* predominantly white. I love most (some) white folks!! It's just hard to live in a place where very few people look like you; it feels unsafe—and in some cases it truly was. And growing up in an environment where you have to let white girls do casual racism at you breaks your spirit after a while. So most Black kids in Frisco spend their free time seeking out other Black kids. In that part of the country, simply being Black was enough of a connection to make best friends. Even if the other Black kid was kinda off, it was much better than being friends with the girls who went on *one* Carnival Cruise *once* and came back, with their sus cornrows, smushing their forearm into mine like, "OMG, look! We're the *saameee* color! 😍"

Whenever you'd run into another Black kid out in them soft suburban streets, it was inevitable that you both would become fast friends. That's how Angel and I linked up. We would ride our bikes and be Black together. We would rollerblade and be Black together. We would watch TV and be Black together. We had a grand ol' time being Black together.

Through the Instagram powers that be, I could see that Angel was living her best, California beachy-breezy life down in Orange County. In all her posts, she was glowing in the peaceful vibes of the Golden State. I wanted to glow with her. When I texted Angel to let her know I was moving to LA, she immediately responded to say she'd been planning a move into LA as well and asked if I wanted to move with her. I couldn't believe it. What a dream! I'd be able to avoid playing Craigslist roulette by moving in with my literal homegirl instead. I was elated. I immediately agreed, and Angel got to work hunting for our perfect landing pad. Within days, she was boots on the ground, battling the bitch that is LA traffic, eating up her precious data to send me video walk-throughs of every apartment she looked at. ¡Increíble!

In order to apply for an apartment, Angel and I had to show pay stubs, bank statements, and/or sign our applications in our virginal blood to prove that we were upstanding citizens who could pay rent on time. I had pretty impressive pay stubs from my job in East Hampton,

whereas Angel had a flush bank account from her wait-
ressing job in Sunset Beach. But we began to realize that
we weren't quite pulling in enough for a cockroach-free
apartment in Los Angeles. Every weekend I'd get shaky
videos of her walking through brightly lit apartments,
waving in the mirrors, showing off the views. And every
weekend, I'd fall in love with every single one of those
brightly lit apartments, all of which cost way more than
what I could pay.

Growing frustrated, I recruited our other Frisco eth-
nic friend, Chereen, to help with the search. Chereen is
awesome. She's part of my Good Girl "Momma Never Let
Me Do Anything" Crew. Chereen and I spent a lot of time
being good daughters together, and her good-daughter
lifestyle turned her into a planner, a problem-solver, and
the friend who figures shit out. So even though Chereen
was still in Texas and had no plans to move to Los Angeles,
she started looking for apartments for us online far more
diligently than we were for ourselves. Pretty quickly,
Chereen pointed out that splitting a three-bedroom was
a lot cheaper than splitting a two-bedroom and maybe we
should consider finding a third roommate.

After a few weekends of falling in love with apartments that we couldn't afford, Angel and I decided to take
Chereen's advice. Angel mentioned that she had a friend,
Monica, who was also looking for an apartment in Los
Angeles. "Dope, let's do it!" I told Angel. If she was a friend
of Angel's, then she was a friend of mine—especially if
that meant we could get a bigger place for cheaper.

At this point, though, I was really finna leave NYC; my knuckles were sore from gripping the corkscrew, and I was tired of the smells. New York stank. Angel had a couple of months left on her lease, so I decided to look for sublets in LA to get the lay of the land early. I turned to Craigslist's mature older sister, Facebook, to find a sublet. This was after everyone got smart enough not to get catfished on the internet but before everyone was smart enough to know that *everybody's* doing catfish lite on their profiles. That everybody's gassing up their lives to look better than they actually are (to be continued).

I found a girl who had a room opening up in her two-bedroom apartment in North Hollywood and was willing to rent to me for a month. She looked nice enough, we had mutual friends, and even though I'd never met her in real life, I thought, *Fuck it*. At this point in my life, I was not yet a Scam Goddess, and growing up in the suburbs had made me soft to the world. But at least working the bar scene in New York City had sharpened me up enough. I'd had them street smarts locked downnnn, so before putting down the deposit, I asked her to send me proof of address and bank statements, which she did right away. When looking to sublet, always get proof of address and bank statements. After getting her stuff, I thought, *Bet, no scammer vibes here. Everything's on the up-and-up!*

One steamy December day in 2015, I landed at LAX ready to goooo. I had my hair did, waist snatched, brows beat, car shipped—I was rea-DY. I hadn't even unbuckled my plane seat belt before I texted my soon-to-be-roomie.

> **Me:** Hey, new roomie! Just landed.
> Excited to meet you!

When I got in my car a little bit later, I put her "North Hollywood" address into my phone only to see it was in Van Nuys. Anyone who's spent time in LA knows that Van Nuys isn't North Hollywood. Van Nuys is so far north that it's basically San Francisco. But Day One LA Laci didn't know this; she was just happy to have a place to stay. As I pulled onto Century Boulevard, I *finally* got a text back from my future roomie.

> **New Roomie:** Hey! Me too. Just so you
> know, the last subletter had to stay a
> bit longer, so unfortunately the living
> room isn't open, but you can come
> get your keys and move your stuff in!

Living room? Isn't open? Move my . . . what is this now? I pulled over and called the subletter. Turns out that when she listed her spot as a "two bed," the second bedroom was actually the living room. Catfish-fucking-lite. I felt *completely* duped. Not only was there still someone living in the room I'd already put a deposit down on, but the room didn't even exist! A living room is not a bedroom, my guy. I told this woman that if she didn't wire me my money back immediately, there would be hell to pay. I already had my car back, and I was not above pulling up on a bitch. Luckily for me, this woman did not want to pay hell and wired me the money instantly. Great, except now, I was in a bind.

When I told Angel about the drama, she kindly offered me a spot to stay at her apartment. "Let's go to happy hour and figure this shit out," she said, which sounded like the perfect way to erase all the bad blood from my bumpy intro to the Los Angeles subletter scene. I put her address in my maps only to see she lived in the middle of the Pacific Ocean. But I didn't care; I was so incredibly thankful to have someone to lean on. My hometown homie, here to save the day. My dreams of LA living would have to wait until the next day . . . or the day after, but at least I was *in* Southern California and had narrowly averted my first scam. I drove down to Sunset Beach in high spirits. Everything was coming up Laci.

I pulled up to the address Angel had given me and was pleasantly surprised to see the epitome of a beachy-breezy California-Dreamin' kind of spot. It looked exactly like every movie about California you've ever seen: No one was wearing shoes. The main mode of transportation was rollerblades. There were even breakdancers spinning on cardboard. I felt like I was in a movie set. As the salty ocean winds washed off my stressful arrival, I nodded to myself. *This will do . . . this will do.*

But when Angel came down, something seemed a little off. She was wearing her traditional hoochie drip—no judgment, I'm a card-carrying hoochie myself—but what was weird was she had on a terrible synthetic wig. It was a mess. Those who don't understand deep Black culture might not get that this is a red flag, but when a cute Black girl rocks a wobbly weave out in public, then you know something is bad wrong in her life. It's kinda like when white girls cut their own bangs in their bathrooms. Like, the danger isn't immediate, but it's lurking. I should've taken this big wig red flag and run in the other direction to look for my third housing option in less than twenty-four hours. But when Angel hugged me, she smelled of my childhood, so I let it go. Can't judge what a Black girl's wearing on her head. It's hard out there on these streets . . . regardless of how scenic and cinematic they are.

When we stepped into Angel's apartment, I was pleasantly surprised to find an adorable and well-decorated spot. Much like her neighborhood, Angel's apartment had a beachy-breezy vibe. Everything was styled in a boho-chic kind of way, where it was hard to figure out if she got the furniture from the Target home section or it just washed ashore, leftovers from a terrible yacht accident. Who am I to surmise the difference? "You can set up here," Angel told me, patting the living room couch. "My roommate's out of town this weekend, so it'll be private and quiet." I was so thankful for Angel in the moment I could've kissed her. "Drinks are on me," I told her as I tore open my suitcase and pulled out my least wrinkled top.

At happy hour, we ordered a couple of sugary (read: cheap) Mai Tais and began to catch up on each other's lives. At one point, Chereen called, but I didn't answer it because it was loud and Angel and I were reuniting. I hadn't realized how much I had missed hanging out with Angel, but again, there were a few times where I had my little moments of "Hmmm."

This was before I learned that I needed to work on trusting my instincts, so I kept hearing these little red flags but just smiled and nodded along. (**Learn to listen to your instincts as early as possible.** You're welcome.)

SCAM LIFE LESSON
Learn to listen to your instincts as early as possible.

For example, she was raving about her new boyfriend, and when she showed me a picture, I was surprised to see an older white man who looked like he worked as a roadie for Mötley Crüe. He did not look to be the finest choice. We're all God's children, but some of us are more like his stepchildren. Angel proceeded to tell me that this middle-aged white dude lived with his mother, or as she put it, "His mother lives with him." I know they make them differently in Southern California, but he's just not who I pictured Angel, a gorgeous Black girl, with. Angel's young and hot! A true specimen. She has one of those bodies that artists want to draw. Sure, she needed a new wig—but don't we all, America? What kind of scheme was this man running, and why was Angel going along with it? I looked up from the glow of her phone showing me that old scraggly man baring its teeth at me, and smiled, saying, "If you like it, I love it!" Which is a phrase Black people say when they neither like it nor love it. (Another one? "Love that for you." Emphasis on *you*.)

Then, the topic of conversation turned to Monica, our soon-to-be third roommate. Angel pulled up Monica's Facebook page on her phone and slid it across the table. I looked through the photos and saw what looked like a cute, young, fun girl. She had light skin, big boobs, and a Golden State bubbly smile.

"Oh, she's cute," I told Angel.

"Well, she's kind of annoying," Angel responded, grabbing her phone back. Her energy struck me as odd—isn't this the friend *you* chose? Angel probably could tell what I was thinking because she quickly followed it up with, "But she's clean and she can pay her part of the deposit."

"Okay, sounds good," I told her. *Roommates are the family your finances choose for you. I'm sure it's going to be fine,* I thought.

After a few more cheap Mai Tais—which were clearly going to be a mistake the next day because who drinks rum and ever wakes up okay—Angel and I headed back to her apartment and crashed pretty hard. I was exhausted from fighting off fraudsters while chasing my dreams, and Angel was exhausted from the Mai Tais. I set up on the couch in the living room, tipsily ignoring the irony of running away from one living room couch-bed and into another.

Before I fell asleep, I pulled out my phone only to see Chereen had left me a voicemail: "Laci, call me back. I need to tell you about Angel." It was too late to call back, I reasoned, while sliding my phone under the pillow. Whatever it was would have to wait until morning. I closed my eyes and drifted off to sleep . . . for about two minutes before being rudely woken up by what sounded like someone trying to break out of Angel's roommate's room. The door swung open, and it scared the shit out of me. I pulled the covers up to my chin, trying to lie as still as possible and hoping the killer had bad eyesight and would miss a Laci-sized lump on the couch.

After a few minutes went by and nothing happened, I started to let my guard down . . . and fell back asleep. Who knows for how long, but in the middle of the night, the ocean air picked up, the door swung open, and I woke up in a panic again. My heart was about to burst out of my chest. It wasn't until the morning that I realized what was going on: it was a hot-ass December day in California, and Angel's only A/C was the open windows. It was actually really lovely, authentically beachy, until I realized the ocean breeze was causing Angel's roommate's door to randomly pop open and slam shut throughout the night. Every time the wind marched her ass through the apartment, the curtains would blow and the door would swing. My heart kept leaping out of my chest because I'd watched too much *Dateline* with my grandma and I was certain this was it: this was how I'd end up on *Dateline*.

The next morning, I was an exhausted mess. *How the hell am I going to chase my dreams if I couldn't even sleep long enough to have them?* Angel hadn't even gotten two steps into the room before I burst out, "Girl, I thought I was about to be murdered up in this bitch!"

"Oh my god, girl, I know," she sighed. "That door."

"It's had me up all night."

"It's so loud," she said, before continuing into this story: "One time, I met this dude at a party, right? And we were gonna hook up at his place, but then I realized he was living out of his car. So I was like, 'Fine, we can go to mine.' When we got here, we started fucking on the couch, and that door kept popping open. I thought we were going to get caught by my roommate. It was wild." Angel walked into the kitchen and poured herself some water.

Yeah, so ... let me run that back for y'all. Because it's a lot and you might've not processed everything in that story: Angel met a stranger at a party and wanted to hook up. Again, no judgment. She went back to his place, which was ... his car. Absolutely no judgment there. She then suggested a better spot, took him back to her apartment that she shares with a roommate. Let me emphasize, we are young, progressive, and horny, honey, I am *not* judging. BUT instead of walking two feet to her *private* bedroom with its own, nonrattly door ... SHE HAD SEX IN THE LIVING ROOM ON THE SAME COUCH THAT I JUST TRIED TO FALL ASLEEP ON (and didn't even have the decency to lie to me about it!). You can only fuck on your couch when you live alone, or at least when the roommate is out of town! Yeah, that's a no for me. I can't live with someone who has those types of decision-making skills. I'm just not consenting to accidental threesomes with a strange dude I don't know. I gave Angel a tight-lipped smile and said, "Love that for you."

I scrambled out of Angel's earshot, pulled out my phone, and dialed Chereen's number. She picked up on the first ring.

"Hey, Chereen, you said you needed to tell me something about Angel?" I blurted out. Chereen went on to share her own saga with Angel over the past month. Turns out, when Chereen got involved with helping us apartment hunt, Angel had reached out to her to borrow money for the deposit. Chereen thought it was strange, but she's a good friend and offered to give Angel the money provided that she follow a repayment plan. "I told her all she would need to do is promise to repay me by signing a contract and I'd lend her the money, but she didn't want to do that."

I couldn't believe what I was hearing. "But I saw her bank statements," I told Chereen.

"Laci, I think she's trying to use you and your money to get to LA," Chereen warned before getting off the phone. I was pissed. I'd been in Los Angeles for less than thirty-six hours and I'd already been scammed twice. I gathered my shit from Angel's sex dungeon/living room and moved back into my car—feeling a lot like one

SCAM LIFE LESSON
Forging paperwork is very easy.

of her apparently random-ass one-night stands. This is when I learned the very important lesson that **forging paperwork is very easy**. All you need is Photoshop and a lack of morals—similar to the girlies who pulled a little scam I'd like to tell you about now.

QUEENS OF THE CON

Stephanie Bailey, her daughter Chianti Bailey, and Stephanie's sister Latonya Bailey Dostaly were a scamming familio who ran cons all around Queens. Their most impressive con, IMHO? Stealing a big old home from a dead man.

Now, there isn't much info known about the Bailey family other than the fact that they did some shady shit to defraud the government out of money. And . . . to be honest? I'm not mad about it. I love these kinds of scams! The fucking government is stealing from us on the daily anyway; why not steal a little something from them? Plus, it's a bunch of girlies running a con on one of the biggest and most broken systems in the world? Yes, love to see it. The future really is female.

What I do know is that in 2014, when I was still white-knuckling my way through my daily subway commute a borough away, Stephanie moved into a beautiful home (with a horrible mint paint job) with her family in the upper-middle-class neighborhood of Laurelton, Queens. Shortly after moving in, Stephanie's daughter Chianti filed a will for Russell Butler, the previous homeowner, claiming she was his heir. Now, I'm not an expert on the whole will-filing process because I'm going to live forever, but I don't think someone you've never met can just file a will on your behalf. But you do you, Chianti: dude's dead anyway, and we all have to be toppling the patriarchy in any way we can . . . even if it's with bureaucratic paperwork. As a result of this filing, Chianti was granted ownership of the home. She just wrote a note like, "Um, actually this is mine. Thanks!" Because of that, Chianti was able to take $200,000 out against the home. Then she got another $100,000 in funds owed to Butler's estate. I don't even know what that means. There are just funds out there? Being *owed* to old dead guys' estates? This home had a whole trust fund and everything. $300,000? Sheesh.

Meanwhile, Chianti's mom, Stephanie, was working on her own side scam, collecting $90,000 from Section 8 housing vouchers, using a fake lease and a faker landlord attached to the home. Don't worry—Stephanie's sis Latonya was also working the system, using her job at the New York City Human Resources Administration to steal the identities of thirty people, mostly children, and filing tax returns in their names. Latonya ended up scamming New York State out of almost $40,000. Let me get this straight: Sister Latonya is doing *the most work*, like she's got an actual job and is filing all sorts of taxes, yet she only pulled $40K? Well isn't that a bitch. Chianti over there was just like, "Um, actually this house is really mine," and she gets six figures. Even defrauding is an unfair game.

This family of fraudsters spent a decade running money schemes before they were caught—Russell Butler's nephews, who weren't too thrilled that three randos were living in their uncle's house, made a phone call. This resulted in Stephanie and Latonya getting picked up, but our girl Chianti remains at large. You go, Chianti. Honestly, this story's cute. There's nothing I wouldn't do for my momma, even if it meant moving into an old-ass house in some boring suburbs to make sure she's comfy.

The thing I love about scams like this is that the two categories of people they were scamming were 1) a dead guy and 2) the whole U.S. government. I'm not a fan of either of those entities, so this is an A+ housing con in my book.

MOSLEY AND THE MELROSE HILLBILLIES

After my second roommate situation in Los Angeles fell through, I was stressing. I didn't have the Bailey family's powers for snatching up homes. *Where the fuck was I going to live?* I want to emphasize that at no point was I homeless or even close to becoming homeless; I wasn't even really couch surfing. But as soon as I get on that Jimmy Kimmel couch, you know my origin story is definitely going to be like every other successful actor's—i.e., "I came to LA with nothing more than my two suitcases and a dream." That's an easy con when it comes to origin stories. **People love struggle, so you have to give them that sprinkle of strife.** All those rags-to-riches actors who were "homeless" when they

---

SCAM LIFE LESSON

People love struggle, so you have to give them that sprinkle of strife.

---

first moved to Los Angeles? They're just crashing with their college homies for a night. And that's the truth.

But I was getting really frustrated at this point. I'd spent my entire life fighting for independence, to be able to live where I wanted and how I wanted, and couch surfing was nowhere in that plan. I turned to the only other person I knew who was looking for an apartment: Angel's frenemy Monica. Provided her pay stubs weren't photoshopped and she was still looking for a roommate, I didn't have any other options. I looked Monica up on Facebook, said a little prayer, and sent a message to see if she was still interested in a roommate.

Monica responded right away saying she was and suggested we meet up at a diner in Pasadena for a vibe check. Once again, I dug through my suitcases, pulled out an outfit that gave off strong live-with-me energy—a Roomie Romper, if you will—and headed to Pasadena to ace that vibe check. You know that people who own rompers close the door when they pee and do not leave their dirty dishes in the sink . . . and nothing says financial responsibility like shorts that are also a shirt.

I recognized Monica immediately; she looked exactly like she did in her Facebook photos: pretty, bright, effervescent. We hit it off. When I told her about everything that had happened with Angel, Monica was horrified, quickly admitting that she didn't even know Angel that well. According to Monica, they were just Facebook friends in an actors' group. Yet another weird Angel lie coming to light.

I instantly liked Monica; she was full of great stories and told me she had moved to LA to pursue acting. *Me too, Monica, me too!* I could feel her excitement for the industry pouring out through her words. Her passion was infectious, and I finally felt like my getting-fucked-over-a-thon was over. Shortly after that meeting, Monica and I moved into a three-bedroom apartment in the Melrose Hill area of LA. All it took was three couches, one sketchy subletter, a failed childhood friendship, and two random roommates, but I did it: I found myself a spot in the City of Angels! *praise hands*

We moved into this huge, old house that was chopped up into condos right on Melrose Avenue, mere blocks from the Paramount Studio lot. Hollywood, baby! I was so used to tiny little New York sardine tins that our standard LA apartment felt like a mansion. The kitchen was big; our bedrooms were bigger—sure, the place looked like it hadn't been updated since the 1980s, but I didn't care: the '80s were in!

Monica and I found our third roommate, Vanessa, on Craigslist, and she was . . . very much a third roommate. Vanessa was in her forties and very grumpy about living with two hot, twenty-five-year-old women. I just want to say there isn't anything wrong with being forty. And Vanessa was gorgeous herself. But if I were forty and living with twenty-five-year-olds, shoot, I'd be grumpy too. Vanessa's mood shifted depending on whether her man, who was—according to her—John Legend's brother, was in town. When he was in Ohio, she was really mean up in the house. When he flew out to LA to "cut John Legend's hair," then Vanessa was chill as fuck. I'm pretty sure the dude had Vanessa on the side and his real family in Ohio. Girl, you've been with this man for *ten years* and he's still in Ohio? You're his mistress, boo boo. But whatever. I was living large in LA, so it didn't matter that I had a hot middle-aged grump creeping around my halls.

Monica and I knew how to have fun together despite Vanessa's negativity, and in fact, Vanessa's anger toward us is probably what fueled our bond. I pretty quickly grew to love Monica for her dreamer mentality. I love dreamers, because I'm a dreamer too . . . Sure, that's a sugarcoated way to say I was just as delusional as Vanessa, but gimme those sweets, honey.

Not only did we get each other, but we had a lot of hot, sexy-women shenanigans together. We liked to shop on Melrose Avenue, aka Shein Street, which had plenty of stores called things like Eden Sky that sold perfect Coachella-worthy fits to wear once and slowly watch as they disintegrate throughout the night. Please remember, when you're young and hot, you don't need designers because your body is doing all the work. I remember this one night, I wore a plastic white dress that looked painted on out on the town, and Monica and I ended up at an Emmy event. Hollywood isn't who you know, it's how you do, and we were doing all right. A white plastic dress is not traditional Emmy attire, but our curves and our confidence got us into all sorts of places we had no business being. We were wild! The world was our oyster! Hollywood babies through and through.

Shortly after I joined a cult most people know as the Upright Citizens Brigade and got really into the improv comedy community, Monica got really into...foreclosures. Even though neither of us had any money, she liked to go to open houses and foreclosure auctions to check out the deadstock. I'd often come home to housing spec flyers laying on the kitchen counter, and it made me love her even more. This girl was such a dreamer that she thought she could be a millennial *and* a homeowner. A *truly* delusional bae.

Monica is the first person I told when I booked my first-ever television role on a half-hour comedy about four close friends trying to scheme their way to the top called *Florida Girls*. (Technically, I had also been an extra in one episode of *Law & Order*, but I'm not counting that for reasons I'll explain later.) After getting The Call, I grabbed a bottle of wine from the fridge, ran to her room, and shared the good news. She was thrilled for me. Her excitement was almost bigger than my own. We popped the Pinot Gris and clinked glasses to a future of fame—all the while being as quiet as possible because John Legend's Brother's Mistress was In A Mood.

The more hours I clocked on *Florida Girls*, the more time Monica spent at open houses and auctions. One day, we were hanging out when Monica said, "Hey, now that you're making TV money, maybe we can buy a house and flip it." She said it all casually like that, as if the thought had just popped into her head. It was clear homegirl had been thinking about homeownership for a while, and even though my gut twinged a little bit, still I thought she had a point. But even though I was making TV money, it didn't mean I *had* TV money . . . yet. I was still in the preproduction process of *Florida Girls* and was terrified of getting fired. There's a popular saying in the biz: "Fire fast, hire slow." I really, really, really didn't want to get fired fast. I laughed off Monica's idea, told her that I didn't have that kind of money, and changed the topic.

When it came time to go film the show in Savannah, Georgia, I realized how close I'd grown to Monica. I was going to miss my hot-girl winglady. I knew she would be fine, living large with her killer hair, big boobs, and Hollywood smile, but it was going to be weird not having her around to dream together. We gave each other a long movie farewell, and I headed up to Georgia to change my life forever.

While I was in Savannah, Monica and I kept in touch with daily texts and occasional catch-up calls. One day, Monica mentioned she was behind on the rent. I was . . . not surprised. How do I put this? Monica was one of those people who, if she'd left her wallet at home and asked me to bring it to her at work, I would not know where to go. She was like Tommy from *Martin*, in that I was pretty sure, most of the time, she "ain't have no job." I wasn't too worried about Mon because I knew she had an old, rich boyfriend who was madly in love with her (even though she was very "eh" about him) and provided a lot of stability and care in her life. See? Monica had that quality about her: she was so sparkly and charming, she could seduce everyone into loving her, including me. So I didn't feel the need to get involved in whatever was going on with her rent.

This is another hot tip for all you baby Goddesses out there: always make sure your portion of the rent payment goes directly to the landlord. That way things are kept clean and cute at the beginning of every month. No mess, no stress. When problems do arise for your roommate, they can figure it out on their own and your hands will be clean. I empathized with Monica and told her that Arturo, our landlord, would probably understand. Monica had been late on rent before and Arturo was always cool with it. No mess, no stress.

Three months later, when I got back from Georgia with my TV money in the bank account, LA hit different. For the first time in my life, I had some coin and I wanted to use it. I booked a trip with my improv team to Vegas so I could spend my "I didn't get fired" money and asked Arturo to come over so we could discuss doing some updates to the house. Maybe get the kitchen looking like the 1990s, or dare I say the 2000s? "I'll pay for it," I said, pretending I was a couple on *House Hunters* who sell artisanal birdhouses but somehow have a $2.3 million budget. When Arturo came over, I walked him through the house to share my vision. "Over here," I told him, "we'd put an in-unit washer/dryer." I walked into the kitchen. "And here," I said, "we'll have granite countertops. The backsplash has to go too, of course, and we need some new cabinets." I felt like I was on HGTV. I just knew when we finished that shit we were gonna *MOVE . . . THAT . . . . BUS!* Arturo politely nodded along until I was done Pinteresting-out on his ass.

"Okay, this all sounds great," he told me, "but first we have to be squared away on rent. I was actually filing eviction paperwork when you called." Hol up, wait a minute. I was gagged. Arturo straight-up sneak-punched me in the throat. Turns out that Monica and Vanessa were *both* behind on their rent and, at times, had submitted partial payments. (I would've never thought to do that—good to know that's a thing, though.) I was all hand on hip, "I leave for three months and it all goes to shit? Nuh-uh. Also, Arturo, why are you sitting on this information and letting me walk around like I'm Oprah?"

Since I was a woman who had recently, against all odds, not been fired from her job, I paid the balance right then and there. But believe me, I did not have a generous loaning policy—or one at all. I turned around, rolled up to Monica *and* Vanessa, and told them both they owed me right away. Monica promised that as soon as she got her next check (but, like, from where, Monica?) she'd pay me back. And Vanessa paid me back that week—but it was still strike threeee for meeee with Vanessa.

Reader, I've been honest with you so far, right? Well, here's the truth about living with John Legend's Brother's Mistress: she was a nightmare and I wanted her out. She was cranky and mean. It felt like living with Squidward, if Squidward was a hot Auntie. So the moment I cashed Vanessa's check, as harsh as it sounds, I took this opportunity to cuss the bitch out and kick her ass to the curb. I was already dreaming up plans to use my TV money to turn Vanessa's room into an audition studio. I told Monica as soon as she got her funds in order and could keep her third covered, I'd cover Vanessa's portion of rent so we wouldn't have to deal with finding a third person who was as ambitious and lovable as us. Monica, as you can imagine, was in full support of this plan.

The future was looking bright, just me and my best-roommate-friend, Monica, living our fabulous LA lives together in that chopped-up mansion. Was it stupid to sign a lease with a person who up until that point had been constantly late on rent? Yes. But I didn't care, I loved Monica and went through hell (Van Nuys) and high ocean water to find her.

After I got back from spending more of my not-getting-fired TV money with my improv cult in Vegas, I was surprised to find Monica's brother had moved into the extra room that I had reserved for our dreams. When I asked Monica about it, she said, "Oh, he didn't *move in*; he's just visiting." *If he's just visiting,* I thought, *why is everything he owns in the room?* Because, you know, if I take everything I own out of my room and bring it to another room, in a different house . . . that's called moving in.

I knew that Monica's brother was . . . how do I put this . . . the archetype of a kid brother: an extremely sweet fuckup. Prior to not-moving-into-but-living-in our self-tape room, her brother had been not-moving-into-but-living-at Monica's boyfriend's place. Her boyfriend even let Monica's brother stay with him *after* they broke up. I do not know what kind of spells this girl was casting, but no ex of mine ever let no family member live with them rent-free. I liked Monica's brother and I know how it goes with family— blood's thicker than water and all that—but it still didn't quite sit right with me. Nevertheless, I'm a reasonable person who has half a soul, so I told her that he was welcome to stay with us until he figured out a more permanent living situation. At the time, I'd actually booked a movie role that was going to be shooting on a remote island for three weeks (more on that laterrr . . .), so I gave him a three-week deadline to find a new spot. Everyone felt that was fair, and I was off, movin' on up, to the next gig.

When that movie ended up falling apart faster than my homelife, I was back in LA two weeks earlier than expected. Of course, Monica's brother was still there, but I'm not a monster. My word is as good as Gucci, so I was fine letting him stay for the full three weeks. But shortly after I came back, I was prancing around the house feeling good about how I was so generously letting *Family Matters* take place in my living room, when Monica tells me that her mom's coming to stay for a bit. Not "Can she stay?" Just "She's coming." It's a lot to have multiple family members that *aren't yours* staying with you for longer than it takes fish to rot, but I tried to be cool with it. Monica's kin were multiplying day by day, but I liked Monica's mom. She was a nice white lady (I always would forget because Monica was biracial) who brought Big Mom Energy with her: cooking, cleaning up after us, complimenting our youth.

One night, I was in the living room watching TV with Monica when her mom and brother walked in, arms loaded with Target shit: new pillows, blankets, closet organizers, decorative pillows . . . If you're staying for only three weeks, why are you bringing home goods into my apartment? I was fine with everything up until that moment. I don't know if it was the brother, the mom, or the up-in-my-grillness of it all, but in that moment, I snapped. It was like in those old-school horror movies where the camera shifts and your perspective on everything changes. Suddenly, it wasn't a few of my roommate's family members in town for a visit; it was "I am paying for a third room, waiving rent for this dude, and these bitches are moving on in like they own the place."

Okay, so when I say "snapped," it was more of a splinter, because I didn't say anything at the time. Just now, years later, and comfortably in my early thirties, I'm beginning to learn not to fall back into my people-pleasing tendencies, to scream and flap my wings when something doesn't feel right like I knew how to do when I was five. But at the time, being in a house with Monica, her mom, and her brother, I just shrank my feelings into a manageable little ball and put them in my pocket.

Later though, when I was telling (complaining to) friends about the situation, they told me, "Oh, you're for sure getting played. You're basically supporting your roommate and her family." I realized that *if* in that three-week period her brother got a single piece of mail addressed to him at our apartment, I was fucked. That's proof of residence right there. Every friend and family member I polled on the situation was like, "Girl, you have to nip this in the bud."

I had been ignoring my instincts, but now the bud was starting to bloom. I had connected with Monica because she was a Hollywood dreamer like me, an actor grinding it out and hoping for a taste of success, but the truth is, in the three years I'd known her, she hadn't done any professional acting. But I had overlooked it because our friendship, her love, was more important than what my body was telling me. The whole open house and foreclosure thing was endearing until my perspective changed and it felt like she was priming me to spend *my* money on *her* dream house. The more I thought about it, the angrier I got. It was clear that a conversation needed to be had. I'd have to cast my people-pleasing tendencies aside and work on my people-confronting weaknesses.

The first moment I could get Monica alone, without her mom or brother hovering nearby, I seized the opportunity. "I feel like," I started as calmly as I could—using my "I feel" statements just like I'd read about online—"I'm getting taken advantage of here." My voice was low and measured. Even though Monica was trying to interject, I continued calmly laying out everything that was bothering me: the brother moving into our dream room, the weird semipressure to buy a money-pit home, the overstaying of her family... and y'all, Monica changed in front of my very eyes. It was like a Dr. Jekyll and Mrs. Hyde moment. She became whichever one is the bad one. Her face twisted and her brows furrowed. Monica did not come at me calm, cool, and collected; she came at me angry, agitated, and fucking ready to rumble.

"Why are you all of a sudden upset with me?" she squealed. "I thought we were friends! Who is in your head, telling you these lies?"

I tried to gain control back. "Just answer my questions," I told her. "When is your brother planning on leaving? Why is there furniture being moved into the room? Are you using me?"

"You're being crazy," she said . . . not answering my simple questions. "You're being crazy." *?!?!?*

To make matters worse, her mom was listening to the brewing argument through our thin-ass walls and decided this was a good time to enter her white ass into the chat . . . This is what turned my splinter into a full-blown snap: I am not about to be financially supporting white moms. Even if they have Black daughters, white moms still scare me. Those ladies are dangerous. So when Monica's mom came into the room with white-level "You're cruising for a bruising" vibes, I'd had enough. What had started as a calm conversation, turned argument between friends, was now snowballing beyond my communication pay grade. "MY DAUGHTER'S NOT USING YOU!" Monica's mom screamed as she came into the room. I stood up and headed out the door because I'm not about to be yelled at in the house I was paying for by a white mom I was paying for, due to her kids that I'm *also* paying for. I'm just not going to fight your mom, bro.

I walked down the hall to my room, all while Monica's mom was screaming at me, "Laci, COME BACK HERE. Laci, THIS INSTANT!" I shut my door and locked it. With my body tense and my heart racing, I stared at the door, waiting to see what would happen next.

When nothing did, I took out my phone and texted everyone I knew about the crazy shit that just went down, just in case a me-sized hole showed up later in the backyard. After numbing out my feelings with the bright light of the iPhone, I somehow managed to fall asleep. After all the adrenaline, my body shut down from sheer exhaustion.

When I woke up the next morning, I called my mom to tell her everything that had happened. I was in the middle of retelling the tale when there was a knock at my door. It was definitely one of those "OPEN UP" knocks and not an "Anybody home?" knock. Sure enough, moments later I heard Monica's voice on the other side. "Unlock the door, Laci! We need to talk." Seconds later came the mom: "Laci, OPEN THIS DOOR RIGHT NOW." More knocking. Even her brother was getting in on the drama with his knocks and his "let's talks." It was a damn mess.

Meanwhile, I've got *my* mama on the other end of the line, hearing this whole fam of blossoming squatters trying to huff and puff and blow my fucking house down. "YOU UNGRATEFUL BITCH!" someone bellowed from the other side of the door. My mama was not having it. "Laci, call the cops," she said, simply and swiftly. Hearing their anger all the way in Texas scared her—which scared me.

The whole situation was giving me *48 Hours*. I always listen to my mom, so I called the cops.

The LAPD showed up ... and immediately came at *me*—not Monica or her mom or her brother but ME—and asked ME to step outside. Beautiful. I called my own personal bullies to the house. Ain't that *about* a bitch? Thank the good Lord, the police didn't believe me right away, BUT they also didn't shoot me! I take my wins where I can. Again, I kept my tone calm and measured and explained that I was the one who called them. When the cops turned their attention to Monica, her brother, and her sister-mom, they packed up and vacated the premises so damn fast they should consider starting a moving company instead of moving *company* into my domicile!

And that was the last time I talked to my first LA friend. At least the ending of our friendship also revealed a commonality: Monica isn't a villain. She was warm, bubbly, just the kind of person you can't wait to tell good news to because you know they're going to be just as excited as you are. My instinct here is still to tell this whole story as an isolated incident and not a reflection of who she was as a person. Because sometimes, when you wrap up future, finances, and family with a friend, things fall apart faster than a Chipotle burrito after the first bite.

Years later, I was celebrating a friend's birthday on the beach in Malibu when out of the corner of my eye, I saw Monica and her brother. I did the polite, adult thing and pretended like I didn't see them. I know they saw me because when they gathered up their things to go, her brother turned to the group of people I was with and yelled, "Don't hang out with her; she's a bitch!" Which is not the polite, adult thing.

As if running into Monica and her brother at one of the hundreds of public beaches in California didn't already seem so random that it might be made up, a couple of years after that I ran into him *again*. This time it was in Hollywood on the street. I didn't even recognize him until he said my name. As soon as I realized it really was him, I braced myself for another unneeded altercation, but he quickly blurted out: "We're really proud of you." "Oh, thanks," I said, a little confused, but touched. It was nice not to be called a bitch this time.

Before I left, he also gave me this gift: "You know," he said, dropping his eyes, "I really *was* trying to move in." So y'all: **Get to know your instincts. Listen to them. Trust them.** I thanked the kid for his service, wished him well, and returned to my apartment—which I can finally afford to live in BY MYSELF.

SCAM LIFE LESSON

Get to know your instincts. Listen to them. Trust them.

Success Scams

Thereis nothing like the scam of success. It's one of the biggest industries out there. There'd be no college without the promise of success. There'd be no stock market without the promise of success. There'd be no marriage without the promise of success. "SUCCESS" IS AN AMERICAN APPLE PIE, WHITE PICKET FENCE-ASS SCAM! No one tells you that *you* define success, and that's by design. The scam of "success" is that it's sold to you as a *thing* but really it's a *feeling*—and you can't commodify a feeling. I wish I had had me to tell me this when I was starting out in the entertainment industry.

Since I was five, I'd *wanted* to be a performer. I wanted it so bad, but I didn't know how to get "it." I knew how to cry on command and how to find my light, but I didn't actually know how to get an audition. The only thing I knew was that I needed a headshot to start. Simple enough. For those who have never auditioned (good for you), a headshot is a

SCAM LIFE LESSON

Always ask for something you want after you've done something to impress the person you want it from.

piece of paper with your big-ass face on it and your address on the back. A lot has changed since I started acting, so maybe people aren't carrying their addresses around on loose sheets of paper, but back when I started, this was very much what you did. And your contact information had better be accurate and updated, because, girl, you don't wanna miss that call! A headshot, in short, is a 2D opportunity to get a casting agent to notice you, fall in love with you, and—eventually—convince producers to invite you to audition.

Yes, that's right, *to audition*. It's only *an application* for an interview. It's also the perfect opportunity for talentless grifters to take advantage of young, ambitious actors. Please, welcome aboard to the first stop on the Hollywood Scam Train!

HEADSHOTS

So, when I first started on my acting journey, I already had headshots from when I was seventeen. In true Laci fashion, I'd figured out that my stellar high school record paired with graduation added up to the perfect reason to badger my mother into getting me a gift. **Always ask for something you want after you've done something to impress the person**

you want it from. So I asked my mom for something every college-bound narcissist wants: headshots.

My mother obliged, and at the end of high school, she took me to a photo studio outside of the Sears in Dallas. I. was. elated. It really felt like my first step toward my dreams, the most professional actory thing I'd ever done, an investment in myself. A few weeks later when I finally got the photos back, I couldn't BAH-LIEVE how good I looked. The photographer had somehow managed to make me, a teenage girl, look exactly like Michelle Obama, a gorgeous, middle-aged mother of two. I was so geeked. I LOVE the Obamas. If Barack and Michelle ever open things up, I'll be first in line. I'm just saying. Give me a call, Barry.

In college, the first time I brought those headshots with me to a play, it became immediately clear that these ain't it. Ah, the beauty of college friends: ready to roast your ass over an open flame whenever possible. I realized that even though my headshots were serving first-lady realness, babes...Michelle is twenty-eight years older than me. When you're a teenage actor, you don't really wanna be photographing like a forty-five-year-old woman—regardless of how regal and beautiful that woman may be. How was I supposed to know that?! I thought I looked mature.

When I got to NYC with those headshots, I knew something needed to change. And luckily, I was in New York City, home to the best photographers in the world! No more left-of-Sears photo studios for your girl. I was going to go to a real-deal professional headshot photographer to get real-deal professional headshots. Where do you find a real-deal professional headshot photographer? The same place you find life-threatening Summer Jam modeling gigs and bitchy third-wheel roommates: Craigslist. I immediately found a guy who could claim the title of "Headshot Photographer to the Stars' . . . Daughters." According to his website, he'd photographed Denzel Washington's daughter, which was enough convincing for me. Great! Nepo me up, Scottie. I reached out to him, and next thing I knew, I was standing in the middle of a busy intersection in Bushwick, dodging traffic and serving face to this photo dude I'd met ten minutes earlier.

In retrospect, the whole situation was kind of sketchy and *definitely* dangerous—but he had one of those foily things to bounce the light just right and kept yelling about how good I looked, so I just went with it. I really began feeling like I was Someone Doing Something. Look at Laci: taking her career into her own hands and making moves. As I changed shirts behind a dumpster in Brooklyn, I thought to myself, *Okay, Laci, this is your time to shine. You serve them face. You serve them youth. You serve them STAR QUALITY!* I popped out from behind the dumpster, feeling like a million bucks . . . and looking like Oscar the Grouch. "Beautiful!" the photographer exclaimed. "Now let's get some of you against that brick wall."

A few weeks and $800 later, I had my gorgeous, edited, real-deal professional headshot photos back, and I was ready to start auditioning. Except, I *still* didn't know *where the auditions were*. Which brings me to grift #2 on the Hollywood Scam Train . . .

CENTRAL CASTING

Even though I had my sleek new pics, I didn't know where to send them. People think "auditioning" is like on *American Idol* where you show up, get in line, and get to do your thing in front of a row of (former?) industry greats. For fucks no. Auditions are kept behind a gate, under lock and key—impossible to find. Most people on the hunt (googling) for auditions eventually find their way to Central Casting. Central Casting is exactly what it sounds like: a catchall website that casts people for TV shows and movies. Now, the only roles they cast people for are what's called "background," so you're literally a human prop. But a toe in the door is a toe in the door. Not having any luck manifesting auditions, I decided that I'd create a Central Casting profile.

When I looked over all the profiles and headshots on the site, I began to realize my headshots—in the middle of the street, up against a brick wall—stood out. At first, I thought that was a good thing: you know, show off my individuality. But after a few weeks of zero bites, nibbles, or even sniffs, I realized that my headshots stood out in the same way clowns stand out.

I had to redo my headshots—a third time—and this time I was going to make sure I went to a real, certified pro. I was going to make damn sure that these were THE LAST headshots I'd ever take. So I asked an actor friend with the best-looking headshots of anyone I knew who she had hired to take hers. When I say "best-looking," I mean her photographer captured her personality on the page. If you were a casting director, tasked to flip through a stack of equally attractive actors, you would've stopped at hers. Maybe it was the radiant twinkle in her eyes or the mischievous way her lips flicked up, or even how her bright shirt popped against the background. Whatever it was, it worked for her, and I wanted it to work for me, too.

As soon as I had the money, I went to the guy she recommended. When I arrived at his apartment, I was excited because I'd never been to a home studio before. I figured he must be pretty legit if he had the space in New York City to build a whole-ass photography studio. I walked into his apartment, and y'all, this man did not have a New York City home studio. It was just an apartment. And a New York apartment at that, so the kitchen was in the living room and the living room was in the bedroom. My stomach twisted into minor discomfort, but I pushed the feeling aside because—like almost every single twentysomething—I still hadn't learned how to listen to my instincts. Plus, he had the foil thing and was saying things like "white balance" and "capture light," so I figured it'd be fine. *Let the genius work, Laci.*

The guy made me crouch near his coffee table, using his sofa as a backdrop, and I served him all the face I could muster from the floor of a stranger's apartment. I didn't feel particularly good about the situation, but at that point, I'd been studying acting for basically my whole life so I knew how to fake it. I locked eyes with the camera like it held the key to the auditions. After a couple of hours, we were both exhausted. He gave me a hug, took my $800, and sent me on my way. I went home and, once again, waited for two weeks.

When I got the edited headshots back, I was appalled. I looked like shit. This was not like the other two times, where I was like, "Oh damn, I'm cute! I can't wait to show these off," and then *later* found out that they didn't work for this reason or the other. These photos didn't work, period. They sucked. My skin looked flat. My eyes looked crazed. I looked like a scared, broke girl, trapped in a gay man's house. How did this happen? How did this man make me—a beautiful, young, blossoming starlet—look ratchet? Then I remembered. How could I have forgotten? My friend is white. The photographer is white. And white photographers do not know how to capture the beauty of Black skin. Don't believe me? Google: "Annie Leibovitz Black People." That woman photographs us like she's saying it with a hard *R*. You can see it in the lighting. Plain as day.

Fuck. I was pissed. I was now $2,400 in the hole, and all I had to show for it was a series of photos that did not capture my personality, did not capture my beauty, did not capture anything. Fuck, man. *Again!* It was really disappointing. With no other options, I posted the new headshots to Central Casting.

Miraculously, even with these shitty headshots, I still got a bite. *Law & Order: SVU* needed background actors for a courtroom scene, and they chose me to be one of them. I couldn't believe it. My first real acting job! I was SO excited. I told everyone I knew. I called home, like, "MAMA! Your baby is going to be on *el televisión*." My first step!

The way Central Casting works is that once you get a request to be a background actor, you basically have thirty seconds to drop all of your responsibilities and arrive on set dressed for the part and ready to go. When I got to set, I could tell right away that Dick Wolf really was getting that *dun dun* coin. No expense spared. I was only there for a half-day and still got an extra rate—which was about one-tenth of what I paid for headshot photos and my Central Casting profile so I was well on my way to making a return on my investment. *And* I got to sit behind Ice-T for the whole shot; you could almost see my entire face. During one of the many breaks in filming, Ice-T turned around and offered me donuts. Ice-T! Me! DONUTS. This was *exactly* what I thought acting would be like: performing with cool people on cool projects.

Since this was my first acting gig, I decided to do it up as seriously and professionally as possible. Really show off all those little-kid acting workshops my mom had bank-rolled in Texas. Every time Ice-T would have a big reaction, I would have a big reaction. Every time he looked confused, I would look confused. Is Ice-T serving surprise? Okay, then, Laci is serving surprise too. I knew the cameras were on me because I was right behind him, so I watched him like a hawk and mirrored absolutely every choice he made—I'm sure it looked insane, but your girl was working. This was my opportunity to get noticed, to get plucked from the background and put in the front row.

When it came time to take a break, I went straight to crafty. *Crafty* is an industry term for "table full of snacks."

I've come to learn that snack quality completely depends on the show's popularity; some crafty tables will have straight-up lobster on them, while others have Pirate's Booty . . . it's always a gamble. Standing around this table, overflowing with free baked goods, finger sandwiches, and drinks—I knew this was the top of pops.

I was crunching away on my mini taquitos, chatting with the other extras standing around the table, when it suddenly dawned on me . . . that most of the extras were . . . how do I put this? . . . batshit. Like legit. There were people there who seemed unwell, as if they didn't really have a proper grasp on reality. Le sigh. Scoping out the crew, it became clear that this isn't where you get plucked. We weren't the talent pool directors were focused on when setting up the shots. We were just . . . extras. Extra bodies to fill seats and to forget about as soon as the scene was finished. I later learned the saying "Background is not the way to the foreground." Oh, is it true. Mean but true!

There are about four stories in Hollywood History where famous, successful actors get plucked out of the obscurity that is background. Four stories out of hundreds of thousands of people . . . maybe even millions. I swear, you have a better chance of winning the state lottery before someone would see you in the background and be like, "You, babe! Put her in hair and makeup. Stat!"

It was a fun experience. I got offered some donuts by Ice-T, and I got paid a whole $95. But coming home that day, I knew in my gut that *this was not the way*. My connection to my instincts was strengthening with every awkward situation. I decided it was time to consult the bigwigs and go straight to the gatekeepers: the casting agents themselves. Welcome to the next stop on the Hollywood Scam Train.

CASTING CONSULTATIONS

Getting a casting consultation is this thing where you pay a casting agent to look over your headshot, watch you perform, and then review your performance using their acute expert opinion for what makes a star. If any up-and-coming actors are reading this, and you take one piece of advice from this book, all I ask of you is: do *not* pay a casting agent to tell you how to act. In fact, let me broaden it up a bit: **do not pay anyone who claims to know the secret to success**. Casting consultations may be the biggest entertainment-industry scam out there, and of course, I was so ambitious, so driven, that I dove right in . . . headfirst, baby!

I found a casting agent online and paid this woman—who mostly casts commercials—to give me her professional opinion on my acting skills. And you know what this bitch told me? "You're acting too Black, and that's not really in style anymore." Not in style anymore? Um, whut? This note fucked me up for years. FOR YEARS. I live with very

---

SCAM LIFE LESSON

Do not pay anyone who claims to know the secret to success.

---

few regrets, but going to this woman—spending time with her and holding her words in my mind, heart, and soul—is one of them. It is so toxic and damaging to tell a young actor—a young *anyone*—to dim their light a little bit, to not shine so aggressively, to not be so vibrant, so glittery, so Black. Never. If you're new and broke and hold very little power in whatever industry you're trying to break into, don't let anyone make a dime off you and don't let anyone taint you with their opinions. **It doesn't matter what anyone thinks. Let them stay in their lane and you focus on yours.**

SCAM LIFE LESSON

It doesn't matter what anyone thinks. Let them stay in their lane and you focus on yours.

STAND-UP & IMPROV CLASSES

A year into my audition search and with no leads to be had, I got some really good advice from an actor friend of a friend *and* it didn't cost me $800. Yet another hot tip for you: when looking for guidance in your career, trust people who are one step ahead of you, not the ones at the top. It's better to consult with people who are still close to the come-up. The actor friend of a friend told me there are basically four ways you can get auditions:

1. Go the school route. Attend a famous performing arts school like Juilliard or Rutgers. Wait until your graduation performance, where agents and managers scout talent, and hope they pluck you out from the crowd. Eventually, those agents and managers will send you on auditions.

2. Go the theater route. Perform for zero money and zero benefits at shitty theaters, work your way up to less shitty theaters, then to good theaters, where agents and managers scout talent, and hope they pluck you out from the cast. Eventually, those agents and managers will send you on auditions.

3. Go the stand-up route. This requires you to write your own material, tell your jokes at the darkest, seediest bars, and practice those jokes until your material gets good. Then increasingly go to better spots and get on a showcase lineup, where agents and managers scout talent, and hope they pluck you out from the lineup. Eventually, those agents and managers will send you on auditions. Note: it may be hard to be taken seriously if you want to be a dramatic actor.

4. Go the improv route. This requires you to find a good improv school (your options are limited) and pay a ton of money to take Level 1, Level 2, Level 3, and Level 4. Then perform at a showcase, where

agents and managers scout talent, and hope they pluck you out from the team. Eventually, those agents and managers will send you on auditions. Please see note above.

I left that meeting amped, fully armed with information. Of the options the dude listed, stand-up was the most affordable, so I chose that route. Even though I was good at stand-up because I know how to write and perform jokes, I burned out pretty quickly because I never felt safe as a woman. Every set felt like an invitation for unwanted attention. There was always some drunk dude hitting on me, some other dude leering at me as I tried to tell my jokes. I couldn't get through a set without at least one person telling me I was too pretty to be funny. I even tried wearing turtlenecks and baggy clothing to be treated professionally—but didn't like hiding my banging body. I was letting the misogyny win a bit, so I pulled back on stand-up and decided to give the second most affordable option a try.

I signed myself up for some make-'em-up classes at the Upright Citizens Brigade in New York—*the* place to go for improv. I arrived with my ugly headshots, paid $400 for UCB 101, and officially entered the UCB program. Another $400 out the door, all in the hopes that someone would tell me where the fuck the damn auditions were. I still had *no clue* where to find an audition or even *find out* about an audition. The gates were sealed shut. For real. I was like Indiana Jones, swinging from my cute little rope, throwing money into the skies, looking for auditions hidden in the Temple of Doom. Is that an Indiana Jones thing? I don't know.

I didn't really click with UCB initially. It was an overly competitive environment where it felt like everyone was constantly fighting for the same costar role on *Broad City*—a role I had zero chance of auditioning for. I thought it'd be warm and collaborative, but it was just cold and cliquey. Sorry, New York UCB, them's just my experiences. I paid my dues and took the classes, but still didn't feel any closer to getting plucked.

When I relocated to Los Angeles to give the whole Hollywood thing a try, I decided I wasn't going to pay-to-play anymore, mainly because I couldn't afford it. Luckily, UCB had a diversity scholarship, so you know my Black ass applied to that shit. I wrote an essay, submitted it online, and shortly after got an email invite to audition for the UCB scholarship. I was thrilled! I'd just gotten to LA and had already found an audition! Sure, it wasn't like a real audition for a real paying acting gig, but it was a start.

So, as you know, I show up to everything approximately five to seven minutes late because five to seven minutes late is on time for me. But this was too big of a deal to fuck around with, so when it came time for my scholarship audition, I made sure to leave my apartment extra early and give myself even more time to find parking, which, in LA, can take anywhere from thirty minutes to three days.

It's true what they say: LA traffic is the biggest bitch in the whole world. So instead of getting there twenty minutes early, I only got there five minutes early—and no one can find parking in five minutes in LA without a miracle. Well, on that very day, the gods smiled down from the big parking lot in the sky, and I found a spot a couple of doors down from UCB . . . right on Sunset Boulevard. Woooweee. Thank you, Jesus.

Now, uh, this area was . . . and remains . . . rough around the edges. Trash everywhere. The U.S. 101 is so close that everything looks, sounds, and smells like freeway. All the people on the street always seem like they're having the roughest day of their life—including former and current UCB comedians shuffling to and from the Sunset location (which is now closed. RIP). It's just a rough 'n' tumble joint. No prettying around it. I was relieved that I found a spot so close by, because I did *not* want to walk through the hood in my full black Ann Taylor suit. Yes, I was wearing a suit. My mama always said, "You have to look your best to play the part." I was looking my best to play the part of a NASA engineer. Whatever. At least I wouldn't be underdressed.

I parked and did a quick check of my makeup in the mirror. Sure, I wasn't twenty minutes early, but I was five, and that's all I need to wipe the sweat from my titties and turn on the charm. I grabbed my shitty headshots—with my new address printed on the back so that anyone who wanted to murder me knew exactly where I lived—and stepped out onto a hot, sweaty LA street.

Immediately, I heard a man screaming in my direction. I figured he was yelling about parking—y'all, I've been towed twelve times, I don't want to talk about it—but when

I checked the sign, I saw that I was in the clear so I shrugged it off and headed toward UCB. But when I turned toward the building, I saw that the yelling man was directly across from me and he looked . . . unwell. I'd been in New York long enough to know that in these types of situations, you have to keep your head down and avoid eye contact, so that's exactly what I did. But as I got closer to UCB, the man— who I was beginning to realize was pretty tall and imposing—got closer to me.

I kept my eyes on the front door of the building, making sure to also track his movements, when he started moving closer toward me and let out an unmistakable: "You bitch, you fucking bitch." *Oh, okay, I'm not just a bitch, but a fucking bitch? I see how it is.* The smart thing to have done in this situation would have been to turn around and run the other way. But this was technically my *first* audition. I'd spent five years trying to get to this point, to audition for something, *anything.* And finally, I'd gotten the chance to audition for the role of "Diversity Scholarship Recipient." So instead of turning around and saving my ass, I barreled toward UCB.

As I gained speed, so did he. Right as I got to the door, the man dove toward me and I tried to juke him. I thought I could hit him with the left and dodge to my right. *Float like a butterfly, sting like a bee, Laci.* Well, I learned that even though I'm scrappy, I don't know how to fight tall, unwell men. Luckily for me, he wasn't that good of a fighter either, because as I tried to football spin around him, the dude kicked me square on the thigh. Right in my Ann Taylor suit. As soon as his boot made contact, though, he lost his balance and fell to the ground. I took that as my opportunity to slip into the building without looking back. Like, BYE.

The second I made it through those doors, I heard, "Laci Mosley? You're up next." Up next meant I had five minutes to run to the bathroom to try to wipe off the big, hulking shoe print from my suit. But standing in the cold, fluorescent light of the washroom, it became pretty clear that the print was not coming off. I had years upon years of street on my pants, and there was no way some soggy brown paper towel was going to clean it off. I desperately rubbed, but the footprint remained, and panic set in. Well, shit. You try to dress up like a NASA engineer to really set a vibe and some old man stomps your ass down to earth.

I headed into the audition with no other option than to quickly explain my cute new fewtprint lewk—and pray that it didn't shift the fun, comedy energy of the room. I walked in, print held high, and explained I was a bit frazzled from my surprise altercation with a drugged-out homie on the street. After everyone on the panel double- and triple-checked to make sure I was okay, one of the interviewees, now a close friend, simply said, "Well, congratulations, you passed our street comedy obstacle course. Now we know you really want this." I laughed. They laughed. The nerves were broken. In that moment, I knew I had found my people and they had found me, too, because later that week, they offered me the full scholarship.

UCB LA was a game changer for me. It was a racket I could get behind. UCB LA was a lot more communal, like a cult; people were quick to pull you into their improv teams and practice make-'em-ups every free moment of every free day. I think people in LA are more inclined to form friendships because everyone is so damn lonely sitting in their cars all day—when they actually get to be around people with similar interests, they white-knuckle those connections with all their might. I got on a house team (shout out to my Mess Hall Homies—I know none of y'all can focus long enough to read a whole book, but I'm sending you love anyway), which meant I got to regularly perform with the most talented people at UCB while getting paid in exposure.

On top of consistently performing in front of important industry folk, I was also on a UCB email list where people shared tips about auditions—the gates were still being kept, but at least now I had made friends who could share some directions to the keys.

One day UCB sent out an email blast looking for comedians to audition for a role that fit my specs. The role was for a new show called *Florida Girls*, written and created by Laura Chinn. Laura Chinn was my improv coach, aka someone higher up in the cult who you'd pay $60 so you could come over to their house and they could tell you how you're winging it wrong. This was nothing like my horrible experiences with casting consultants in New York because Laura was a UCB comedian and improviser herself. She was in the trenches with us . . . many steps ahead and lucky for us willing to show us the map!

It is extremely rare that someone writes, sells, and stars in their own show. Everyone at UCB was thrilled for Laura, but we also knew that she had very little control over who would be cast in her show, so it was time to work. After almost six years, I'd finally gotten the opportunity to submit a real audition for a real acting role on a real show.

I went over to my UCB friend Priscilla's house to put myself on tape (which is also kind of a scam because you're expected to be an actor, director, producer, cinematographer, and editor just to get an audition). Priscilla had a dope self-tape setup with a piece of wood that she used as a backdrop and I thought the rustic feel was perfect for the role of Jayla, a Florida girl with Champagne tastes on a malt-liquor budget. Even though Jayla had some different life experiences than I did, I really saw a lot of myself in her as a character. She wanted the finer things in life and was willing to work for them. Just. Like. Me. I put myself on tape, sent my audition through to production, and didn't give it a second thought. It may have been my first real audition, but I'd been around long enough to know it was not time to get excited or even think about getting excited.

When I got a call asking me to come in for a producer session . . . I honestly couldn't believe it. A producer session *is* the time to get excited: it is the final step in a series of steps before you get *the part*. I'd somehow leapfrogged from putting myself on tape to getting to the last round of auditioning. If this sounds confusing, that's because it is. That's how gates are kept . . . confusing as fuck.

There are usually three classes of people at the chemistry reads: one who is perfect, one who is almost right but physically off, and a nepo baby. I knew right off the bat I wasn't the nepo baby, so I was either perfect or all wrong. 50/50 odds. I'll take it!

Sitting in the poorly lit office building, trying to stop my knees from shaking, I ran through my lines in my head. A tall office assistant with a booming voice and a baby face asked if he could get me anything to drink. At the time, I was obsessed with coconut LaCroix—production offices run on LaCroix; it's what fuels writers' rooms—so I asked for one of those. On the house, so why not, right? He gave me a nice smile and said, "I'll check." A few moments later, the tall office assistant came back clutching a lemon LaCroix in one hand and a lime one in the other. "Sorry," he told me. "We only have lemon and lime." He held both cans out to me. I scrunched my nose, rolled my eyes, and said, "That's okay. I'll drink my spit instead."

SCAM LIFE LESSON

When you're scared, try to charm 'em all to death.

This got a laugh. Which is my main goal in every situation. **When you're scared, try to charm 'em all to death.** The office assistant, still chuckling to himself, led me into the audition room and, much to my shock, took a seat behind the casting table. Turns out, he wasn't the office assistant: he was Tony Hernandez, the founder and CEO of Jax Media, aka the head honchos who were producing *Florida Girls*. Oooo girl, oops. Well, Tony loved my sassy Black ass. I got the part, and I'm pretty sure it's because I made fun of him.

After I got the job—without an agent or a manager, mind you—I barely had enough time to celebrate my first real step into my dreams before Laura called me. "I wrote this role for you," she said somewhat seriously. "I couldn't tell you in case you didn't book it."

"What?! Oh my God!" As if I couldn't get more excited. But Laura cut through my excitement with her honesty.

"I need you to really work on your character because this is Hollywood. If you don't kill it at the table read, they can fire you," she warned.

"Right, yes. You know I'm going to kill it," I told her, but Laura wasn't done.

"If you don't kill it while shooting the first episode, they can fire you."

"Yeah. Totally."

"If you don't kill it while shooting the first few episodes, they can fire you."

"I could go upstairs and never come back, just get Judy Winslowed right out the bitch," I realized.

"Exactly."

"Like a dark-skinned Aunt Viv replaced with a light-skinned Aunt Viv situation."

"Yup." Laura sighed. She knew better than anyone how brutal it is in these Hollywood streets. Nothing is guaranteed. I took a deep breath, thanked her, and got off the phone. STILL EXCITED BECAUSE I BOOKED THE PART AND YOU HAVE TO CELEBRATE WHEN YOU CAN IN THIS HORRIBLE INDUSTRY.

So in the end, did I need to get my headshots retaken three times, spend money I didn't have to upload those shitty photos to Central Casting, and split donuts with Ice-T to get my first real acting gig? No, not even at all. I even booked the role without an agent or a manager, which is pretty unheard of. The whole time I was writing checks to all the predatory agencies promising to "help" with my acting career, I was too ambitious, too goal oriented, to stop and evaluate who I was giving my hard-earned money to. Hell! I showed Laura this chapter before the book was released and she said this conversation was completely different. She was just giving me feedback and honest notes. I agree. Occasionally, the "Scam Likely" call is coming from inside the house! Sometimes need makes us unreliable narrators. She never said I was going to get "fired," but my fear did. When you have a dream so big, so wild, and so improbable that you'll do *anything* to achieve it . . . you stop thinking straight. Just like the woman in this next Hollywood scam.

SHONDA CRIMES

The problem with wanting success so bad that you're willing to stop at nothing for it is that once you actually achieve that success, it can all come crumbling out from under you. Around the same time I moved to LA to continue pursuing my acting obsession, Elisabeth Finch had just secured a dream job writing on *Grey's Anatomy.* Entertainment-industry writing jobs are kept behind the same gates as acting roles, so writers also need to figure out a way to get the key.

After writing a harrowing essay for *Elle* about her battle with a rare form of cancer, Finch was rewarded with a cushy spot in the writers' room on *Grey's Anatomy*. I know I don't need to explain what a big level up this is for any writer. During her five-plus years as the "star writer" for *Grey's Anatomy*, Finch—friends call her Finchie, but I'm not going to do that—continued to write essays and share wild stories about her medical struggles: her bone cancer would go into remission and then pop back up again; she had an abortion while going through chemo; doctors replaced her knee "by accident"; her abusive brother died by suicide—just all sorts of trauma in this lady's timeline. Of course, her struggles were not the kind of thing a friend or coworker would fact-check, because, um, no one wants to be *that* monster. Plus, she was actually showing signs of deterioration.

Of course, when someone goes through so much tragedy at such a young age, there's very little silver lining to be had, but Elisabeth was a writer who'd experienced a lot of medical trauma at a time she was writing on *the* #1 show for medical-trauma porn—so at the *very* least she was making bank to pay for all those medical bills. Elisabeth's rare cancer diagnosis, along with a few of her other medical traumas, even made it into the show, as did she . . . starring in the role of: Nurse Elisabeth. I bet she didn't even need to go through the UCB cult to get that spot, either.

In 2019, the trauma train kept on rolling when Finch went to Arizona to seek treatment for the abuse she'd suffered at the hands of her brother. At the treatment facility, Elisabeth met

Jennifer Beyer, a nurse who had escaped and was recovering from an abusive marriage.

The two fell in love and decided to get married shortly after they met, in February 2020. This is when Elisabeth's whole con came crashing down. COVID hit the month after the two wed, and well, Jennifer had a lot of time to cyberstalk her new wife. Which, like, Jen? Seriously? You didn't think to do your timeline due diligence before putting a ring on it? I'll let it pass, girl; you were juggling a lot.

The more Jennifer saw, the more she realized the math was not mathing. Jennifer, with her medical background, noticed that in the photos of Elisabeth's chemo treatment days her eyebrows and eyelashes were still intact. E-LIS-A-BETH, you have got to shave it alllll if you're going to cancer con! Also what are you doing trying to lie about medical shit to a nurse? A rusty ruse!

Well, after failing to get Elisabeth to tell the truth, Jennifer EMAILED SHONDA RHIMES and texted the showrunner of *Grey's Anatomy* with a simple message: "Please stop letting Finch tell 'her stories' anymore, because they're other survivors' stories." Jennifer is classy AF—my message would not have had the word *please* in there, I'll tell you that much.

You can imagine how that went over with Disney HR. You can't? Well, they immediately tried to open up an investigation, but Finch took a leave of absence, which is white businesslady talk for "you can't fire me; I fire you!"

The worst part about Elisabeth's whole grift is . . . I completely see where this bitch was coming from. I don't condone it, but I do understand. Don't tell anybody, but shit's hard out here in Hollywood. It is I-M-P-O-S-S-I-B-L-E to get noticed sometimes.

Everyone who works in Hollywood needs attention. The more attention we get, the more successful we become. It's pretty fucked up.

THE SCAMCRET TO SUCCESS

Success is *such* a scam because it's always a moving target. Every piece of advice to young actors is always about getting an agent who will help you find auditions. I spent years trying to get noticed by agents and ended up getting cast in a TV series without one. The line between failure and success is a thin, squiggly one . . . and I've learned not to pay too much attention to it.

America has taught us all to want "success" without clearly defining what success really is or how it changes from year to year, person to person, job to job. Scam artists prey on people's wants—the more you want something, the more you open yourself up to scams—and when you want something as nebulous as success, well, you're kind of an easy target.

Just know this: mistakes are made when you don't monitor your need for success. Mistakes are made when you're single-minded. Mistakes are made when you *only* focus on your own advancement and don't stop to actually, authentically connect with those around you. But I guess mistakes are made no matter what you do—lol—so make sure to surround yourself with some good-ass friends, keep your wits about you, and best of luck out there.

Friendship Scams

Speaking of good-ass friends ... I've never had trouble making friends, but I *have* had trouble with boundaries—mostly people understanding mine (honestly, including myself... lol). I guess that's what happens when you're the oldest in a family and you've been programmed to please. Sure, "boundaries" is a buzzword in this era of TikTok Therapy, but it's wild how often they're the culprit in almost every social situation that stresses me the fuck out. Boundaries are a real thing to pay attention to, y'all. The evolved and enlightened girlies know that boundaries help foster healthy relationships, yet they can feel impossible to implement. We are never taught *how* to engage those motherfuckers, and even if we do figure out how to set "healthy boundaries," it's often seen as cold or rude because this country is uncomfortable with women who advocate for their needs, especially when those women are Black. And yet, boundaries are crucial to our progress as functional human beings.

My first inkling that I maybe had an issue with boundary setting was in elementary school. I went to Akin Elementary, y'all remember? The place I went missing from. The yellow and blue school colors are still seared in my brain today, mostly because we had to wear uniforms that matched. Even though collared shirts and pleated skirts were hardly a fit one would want to rock at Fashion Week, I kind of liked wearing a uniform. Uniforms evened the playing field when it came to the little-kid hierarchy. No one was showing up in Gucci. Kids didn't feel ashamed about what was happening at home—we were all equals in the same ugly shit. Sure, the uniforms limited our freedom of expression, but that means we had to rely on our personality, babes. I swear, wearing uniforms in elementary school forced me to invest a little more in the impression I left on people.

Jasmine was an Akin Elementary heavy hitter with the winningest of personalities. I met Jasmine right when I was coming out of my innocent, whimsical Junie B. Jones era of life. I was starting to notice boys, and Jasmine had a boyfriend at another school, which was fascinating to me. A boyfriend! At another school? What a thing. That's like taking a lover in Europe to an elementary school kid. Even though we were really young, I already could feel that Jasmine had a superior quality compared to other kids our age because she had somehow convinced someone—who wasn't her mom—to love her. I wanted to know what that superior quality was. So I quickly became friends with her to find out. I started sitting next to her at lunch and making sure we were partners in gym class. And we would always coordinate outfits . . . okay, we were wearing uniforms, but still: CONNECTION!

One day, during reading class—I think they called it reading; it can't really be called English when you barely know how to read—I was caught passing a note to Jasmine. You know, to help her with her reading. My teacher snatched the note from me and squinted at the writing. My loving mama says I had the handwriting of a doctor, but really, I have the handwriting of a serial killer . . . (You're lucky this book is typeset.) Seriously, my writing is so bad that if you got two letters, one made up of threatening words clipped from magazines and one normal note from me, you'd call the cops about mine first. My teacher, unable to actually read what the scrap of paper said, folded it back up and gave me an icy, "Laci, please come to my desk after class." Ooh, I still have goose bumps at the back of my neck. I hate being in trouble. Even though my teacher couldn't quite make out what the note said, one word was extremely legible and very clear. That word was *SEX*. Needless to say, she sent the note home along with a write-up that required my mother's attention *and* signature.

At pickup, I stress-paced until my mom appeared. Unable to handle my guilt for one more second, I handed over my teacher's note. My mother, who had a better handle on my handwriting, read the note aloud: "Did y'all do freaka sex?!" She looked up from the note, trying to hide her laughter. "Laci, did you write this note?" I looked down at the cement and nodded, doing everything in my power to minimize the amount of trouble I was about to get into.

Okay, hear me out: I was completely justified in my freaka sex question. I'm telling you! Jasmine was in elementary school. She had a *boyfriend*. She was *worldly*! I wanted to know what they were doing and how they were doing it! I would give you the details I learned here, but Jasmine never even had a chance to attempt to decode my scrawlings so I never got an answer. But that didn't matter because my mom had questions of her own.

"How do you even know about sex?" she asked while scribbling her name at the bottom of the note.

"From listening to Usher songs and watching *Living Single*," I responded because it was the damn truth. This moment marked the last time I was allowed to listen to Usher or watch *Living Single*. I should've lied. At the end of the ordeal, my bad grammar got me in more trouble with my mother than the note itself. Which was a relief because Jasmine was my homie and I *did not* want to give up my blossoming friendship with her.

One day, Jasmine and I were heading to lunch when she mentioned that she didn't have money that day. "I got you!" I piped up. I was thrilled for an opportunity to show Jasmine how much she meant to me. Paying for a meal? Great! Maybe I'd be her boyfriend next. When Jasmine told me she couldn't pay for lunch, it broke my heart. And looking back now as an adult, the whole lunch-money situation in this country *really* gets my blood boiling. Like, we're putting kids in an educational prison, not allowing them to leave the four walls of their schools, *and* we don't give them a hot meal without charging them? Come on. Don't get me wrong—I love education! But I also think if you're *making* kids go to school (as you should), you should also be making them a tasty meal.

I knew I had to do everything in my power to get Jasmine the money she needed to eat. If roommates are the family your finances choose for you, then friends are the family that *you* choose for you. The complicating factor about this was that I was nine and had zero concept of or access to money. "We can split lunch today, and I'll bring you lunch money tomorrow," I concluded.

When I got home, I checked the couch cushions, under the bed, anywhere I could think money would be stored. And then I heard my mom come home. I *heard* her come home because she had this enormous black Coach purse that was always jingling with change. When I close my eyes, I can still hear the sound it made as it hit the floor. I don't really understand why my mom was carrying around so much damn change. Maybe it was because it was the late nineties and that's just what businessladies did? Maybe she wanted to make some wishes at the water fountain at the mall? Maybe she was saving up to buy a tollbooth? Who knows. The lady was a walking Coinstar. Anyway, that jinglejangle alerted me to an opportunity: I was going to rob my mother. A great plan. Doing bad to do good. What could go wrong?

Sometimes you gotta do bad to do good.

To be honest, I still believe that **sometimes you gotta do bad to do good**. So while my mom was getting dinner ready, I grabbed a handful of change and snuck it into my backpack, putting each coin in a different compartment so they wouldn't clink together. Little Laci was smart, generous, *and* sneaky.

The next day at school, I showed Jasmine my loot and her eyes lit up. "Thanks, Laci!" she squealed before giving me a big hug. My body filled up with the warmth of a good deed, like, *Shoot, maybe I don't even need my own lunch money anymore. My stomach is full on friendship.* The next day, I brought Jasmine another handful of my mom's purse change. I continued to bring her handfuls of change until my mama stopped jingling when she came home. One day, shortly after my mom realized that her purse was too light and too quiet, she confronted one of the two people living in the house at the time: me.

"Laci, have you been stealing change out of my purse?" she asked, arms crossed, face twisted into a frown.

I wilted immediately. "Yes, I was taking the change." I have no backbone when it comes to my mom. I got in trouble—big trouble. Trouble at my mom's house meant I had to write an essay based off a mother-assigned chapter from our set of Black History Encyclopedias. Did y'all know the kings of Nubia conquered and ruled Egypt for about a century? Because my little thieving ass did.

The next day, I had to tell my bestie, Jasmine, with the freaka sex boyfriend that I didn't have any purse coins for her. I was sweating. I really loved being her friend, and I didn't want to disappoint her. I worried that if I disappointed her she would withdraw her friendship. This is something I'm still battling today: that fear of disappointing people. It's the curse of being a people-pleaser. We're so scared of losing love, we'd rob our own mamas just to keep it.

When I finally worked up the courage to tell Jasmine that the purse-money pipeline had dried up, Jasmine—to my surprise—did. not. care. at. all. "Oh, that's fine!" she said, after which she promptly went to buy her own lunch with her OWN MONEY. Turns out, Jasmine didn't need my mama's purse coins at all. She was just *using* me for some extra quarters and dollars. And I don't blame her—after all, I was freely offering them to her!

So what's the lesson here? Hm? Well, we should all help our friends, *of course*. But it's not our responsibility to full-on insert ourselves into problems no one asked us to fix. If you want to volunteer, do that. But when it comes to friendships, be careful about pouring too much of yourself into something that's not meant to be. Jasmine never even asked for my help. Walk it back to the top of the chapter. Jasmine never explicitly asked for me to pay for her lunches. But my brain (and also probably your brain) thought she asked. She didn't. She was just sharing that she didn't have money for lunch that one specific day.

I'm all for support. It's beautiful to show up for friends, even when they don't ask you to. It's important to step into the gap when people are suffering. But before you step into that gap, take a moment and make sure you're not pouring in too much of yourself. Because if you pour too much of yourself in, there might be nothing left behind. This is something Johnathan Walton had to learn the hard way in the scam I'm about to tell you about.

THE BAD BITCH OF BUNKER HILL

In 2013, a few years before I started my own saga with the shitshow that is the LA rental market, Marianne "Mair" Smyth was scrounging around Downtown Los Angeles, looking for her next victim. Mair, who *also* goes by Marianne Welch, Marianne Andle, and twenty-three other aliases because scammers like a cute identity change moment, first showed up in the Bunker Hill neighborhood of Downtown LA. Bunker Hill was initially built for some rich dude in the late 1800s and lined with lavish Victorians that eventually fell into disrepair a few decades later. Victorians are expensive sons of bitches, so the homes were chopped up and turned into apartments—a common practice in Los Angeles. Soon, the neighborhood, filled with brothels and ramshackle cribs, became known as Hell's Half Acre. It was a really seedy area in an even seedier part of the city. But, and I'm glazing over a few details here, these days Bunker Hill is home to the Museum of Contemporary Art and a number of high-end restaurants and overpriced coffee shops. The dilapidated Victorians have been replaced with expensive high-rises, catering to lawyers, producers, and other moneyed scam artists in the area. Perfect for a woman like Mair, aka the Queen of Con. When Mair arrived on the DTLA scene, she had been conning people for decades, and her victims included mentally ill navy dudes, the elderly, and even her own daughters. But one victim, Johnathan Walton, did not go quietly into the night—he fought back.

Johnathan, a reality-TV producer who has worked on shows including *My Crazy Ex* and *Shark Tank* (aka what your suburban homies love to watch to black out from after a stressful day of humaning), met Mair after a building-wide meeting to address the horrendous trauma of losing access to their Olympic-size pool. That pool was the building's community gathering space, an oasis in the middle of DTLA. When a group of tenants met up to figure out how to win it back, Mair immediately stood out from the others: she was confident, charming, and knew how to command the room with her presence. Not only did she tell dirty jokes to lighten the mood (my kinda bitch), but Mair gave the tenants a solution that would alleviate the Olympic pool injustice: her rich boyfriend, a powerful politician, could use his sway to lobby to win the water back for the building.

Sometime after the meeting, Mair invited Johnathan and his husband out for dinner—a dinner that she paid for and during which she began to plant the seeds of friendship. Mair told Johnathan about how she was an Irish heiress who had been disowned by her family back in Ireland. Her story really resonated with Johnathan, especially because his family had disowned him when he came out. She also shared that even though she was extremely wealthy (and about to be wealthier when her €5 million portion of her "royal Irish uncle's" inheritance would come through), she worked at luxury travel agencies because she loved selling vacations "in the Pacific Islands." Yeah, okay, so all the Irish shit was bullshit—bitch was from Maine—but apparently, she really did work at a luxury travel agency. It didn't matter what was fact or fiction, Johnathan swallowed it all whole. "I loved her like a sister," he later told reporters.

As their friendship blossomed, a concerning figure entered Mair's life, her "evil cousin," an "Irish barrister" who was dead set on keeping Mair from her inheritance. Johnathan said he even saw emails and texts from Mair's cousin threatening her. According to Irish Royal Law (a thing that doesn't exist), Mair could be disinherited from her €5 million inheritance if she were convicted of a felony. Mair showed Johnathan a very convenient email where her barrister warned her of the law. Johnathan, who had ten years of journalistic experience covering stories where people murdered their moms to get at some of that dead-lady money, grew concerned for Mair. Oh, Johnathan, you sweet, kind man. There you are, stepping into the gap. I get it: the gap is a compelling place to be.

One day, Johnathan got a call from Mair, who had been "arrested" because her evil cousin "set her up," and she asked if he could please bail her out. Mair was "his sister," after all, so he sent the thousands of bail dollars immediately. This is what I like to call the "I'm good for it" con. It's people who are constantly asking for favors (mostly money) and promise you up and down that they're good for it—and sometimes they are . . . but eventually they won't be. So if you ever hear a pal ask for a favor, followed immediately by "I'm good for it," run the other way.

Mair did, actually, pay Johnathan right back. So she really was "good for it" that time. But, like all "I'm good for it" folks, Mair called Johnathan again and asked to borrow money for a lawyer—$50,000 this time—and Johnathan, God bless the guy, helped her out. So bail turned into $50K, and then it turned into a retainer fee and then rent money and grocery money—and just when Johnathan thought the case was almost over (and he'd start to get some of his money back), Mair was arrested once again.

Devastated that his friend was in jail, Johnathan—against Mair's wishes—decided to go visit her to offer moral support. When Johnathan hopped onto the jail's website to set up an appointment, he found out that Mair was in jail for felony grand theft . . . not at all the evil-cousin "setup" that Mair initially said she'd been arrested for. Finding out that a close friend who you had assumed was a victim of some false accusations was actually in jail for stealing money is not a fun thing to discover when you've sunk $92,000 into the relationship. Johnathan finally figured out that Mair was grand thefting him, too.

The thing I like about Johnathan is that most people, when they're scammed to this extent, tend to curl up in a corner of shame and hide from the world. But not Johnathan. He went right to the police, and you know what the cops did? Nothing. Fucking LAPD, man. But even this didn't deter Johnathan. Instead, he put his years of producing and journalistic experience to use and created a podcast about his experience. Johnathan, my man! I see you, boo: keep doing what you're doing!

Since starting a blog and a complementary podcast called *Queen of the Con*, Johnathan says numerous people who were also victimized by Mair have reached out. To date, there have been about forty victims spanning the globe from Ireland to Tennessee who have come forward to share that they too have been victims of Marianne Whateverthefuckhernameisnow's fuckery. According to the people who have shared with Johnathan, Mair has pretended to have cancer, has pretended to be a celebrity psychic, has surgically changed her appearance to avoid getting caught, has married for money multiple times, has run mortgage scams, and more. Even though she was arrested in 2018 for what she did to Johnathan and all the others who managed to get the police to investigate, she was released in 2020 because of COVID. And though the po-po say they know where Mair currently is, I doubt it. So keep your eyes peeled for a plastic-looking, cancer-faking, Irish-royal, psychic travel agent who wants to be your friend.

I sometimes think friendship scammers are the laziest ones of the bunch. It is in our animalistic instincts to feel like we're a part of a group, that we belong in a crew. Humans need community. Preying on people's need to belong and taking advantage of their kindness are too easy. That's why I prefer bigger cons, like ripping off the government or fucking over systemic racism—that's a better focus for one's scammer talents, in my opinion. If you ever come across a friendship scammer, someone who drains the people around them to grow stronger, richer, more powerful, I say you take a page out of Johnathan's book and put them on blast for all to see and all to avoid.

HOLIDAY WIN

While I was in the middle of writing this book, something happened that felt like a perfect encapsulation of another aspect of the scams of connecting with other people. I decided to include it, but I need you to walk with me here. It's messy.

I was hanging out with my close friend Kyle. I know Kyle basically the same way I know all of my friends, through the cult of UCB. Kyle is just one of those friends who is always there for me, and I'm always there for him. I try not to let a lot of people see me when I'm not fully composed and in control, but Kyle is one of those people I can truly be my own, messy self around. One time, I burst into his apartment, unannounced, to have an anxiety attack on his couch. Without skipping a beat, Kyle turned on *Drag Race*, and we watched our girls werk until I got my breathing right again. So yeah, Kyle's a very close friend.

My apartment is a few blocks away from Kyle's, which is a mini adult-friendship miracle. When we get bored of each other's couches, we like meeting up at this swanky old Hollywood bar at the bottom floor of an ornate, historic Hollywood hotel in our neighborhood. Not only does the bar have good drinks and a sexy vibe, but I ran into Malia Obama there once, so I really like going there to relive the moment in time when I was an arm's length away from someone who shares DNA with my boy Barack.

A few weeks ago, Kyle and I met up to go to our bar, only to realize it was Sunday and the bar was closed. I get it: day of rest. I'm not mad, but we really wanted to tie one on. So we decided to go to another bar down the street that happens to make some A-plus martinis. Martinis always feel very *Sex and the City* to me, but really, you're just drinking three ounces of straight-up liquor with a splash of olive juice in a fancy glass. Whatever, we felt cute. Kyle and I had a couple of martinis and were feeling properly Sunday early-evening tipsy when we decided to walk back to my apartment for a nightcap.

As we got closer to my apartment, I noticed a woman who stood out from the rest of the block because she looked like me. I live in a gentrified neighborhood and there aren't a lot of Black women around so, you know, I notice when there's another one of me nearby. This woman was also short like me. (I'm 5'9" on the internet, but 5'1" in real life.) And she seemed young like me.

"Hey," I told her as we walked up to my place, "do you need help getting into the building? Or . . ." I trailed off, giving her space to fill in her needs.

"No," she said in a small voice. Up close, I was struck by how much younger than me she was. "I'm trying to get to a shelter in Venice." Kyle is a gay man from Boston, and I'm a sort of gay person from the South. We both know what it's like to live in unsafe environments, which meant we could not walk past this woman without offering to help her out. As soon as she mentioned the shelter in Venice, Kyle and I sprang into action: this was something we could work with! Kyle started calling different shelters, while I ran to a nearby ATM to pull out some cash so she could pay a cab to get her to Venice, which was so far from where I lived it was basically a different state. Cash in hand, I headed back toward where Kyle and the girl who looked like me were standing. I noticed that she had moved slightly farther away from where Kyle was pacing and making phone calls. I clocked this and handed over the money. "Here," I told her. "This should help get you there." She graciously took the cash and tucked it into her jacket.

After many calls, Kyle told us, "All the shelters in Venice are either all-male or booked." Out of the corner of my eye, I could see her disappointment. "That's okay," I said. "There are plenty of hotels around; I'm sure one of them will put you up."

I suddenly remembered our favorite bar was inside the swanky old Hollywood hotel. "Kyle!" I yelled, thrilled with my own idea. "The bar!"

"Oh my god, yes!" He yelled back. We were vibrating with the excitement of a good deed. We both turned to our new friend and giddily told her we could take her to a great hotel where she would be treated like a queen. That way she could rest, regroup, and figure out her next steps in the morning.

The three of us headed down to the hotel—which I'm being intentionally vague about because I love you, but I don't want to see you at my spot—and as we walked in, I could tell just by looking at the clerk's face that there was zero chance he was going to rent a room to us. And sure enough, he didn't. Kyle and I had momentarily forgotten that it was Pride and all the rich gays had descended on the swanky local hotels. There was no way we were going to find a nice hotel room in the Hollywood area. But you see, the problem is, we were *in it* now.

So I ordered an Uber to the nearest motel because walk-ins are usually welcome. The three of us got in, and before I knew it, we were taking our new friend, who neither of us knew, to a second location. During the drive, our friend told us her name was Hannah, she was twenty-two (so young!), and she had just gotten to the city from Chicago. She seemed relieved when we arrived and approached the desk.

"Hi, I'd like to book a room for two weeks," I told the man behind the counter. The clerk looked me up and down, then he looked Kyle up and down, and then he looked Hannah up and down. It was a lot of up and downs, and neither direction was in our favor.

"We're all booked up," he finally said.

At this point, Kyle and I had decided Hannah was our daughter and it became our main goal to get her to safety. I pressed on, "You don't have *any* rooms available?" The clerk shook his head no. So I went full white lady on him: "Can you please call your boss? I don't understand how this is possible." To his credit, dude called his boss, and after a little performative back-and-forth, the clerk told us that he actually had a room available, but only for one night. "Fine," I said, "book it."

Without a response, he began poking away at his keyboard, and then he sighed again. "So sorry, we just got an online booking, so she can't stay." I rolled my eyes knowing that there wasn't much further I could push my anger without us having an even bigger problem and headed toward the door. Kyle was already back on the phone with another motel as I opened my Uber app. Kyle smiled into the phone. Success? "Okay, great, thanks so much. We'll be there soon." Success. On to the third hotel it was.

I ordered another Uber, and this time I got in on the passenger side because I like to pretend I'm a tall person. Hannah got in the back and Kyle followed her. "Um, is it okay if I sit on the outside?" Hannah asked, her voice the strongest it'd been all night. "Oh my God, yes," Kyle said. He immediately hopped out of the car and waited as we rearranged ourselves so that Hannah could be next to me and next to me only. Kyle and I gave each other a quick look because we both realized the situation had just gotten a lot more delicate. It was clear that Hannah didn't want to be near men, even the gay ones, so we had to be gentler because we had accidentally kidnapped a twenty-two-year-old stranger. Kyle and I grew quieter and quieter, probably both realizing what a fucking comfort bubble we'd been floating in. Here I was, a person with tons of resources, money, support, recognition, and even I couldn't book a hotel room, couldn't even find Hannah a place to stay for one night? It felt impossible to get a roof over her head, even a temporary one.

Once we got to the desk and explained the situation for a third time, the clerk clacked into his keyboard only to say, "Actually, we don't have a room for you." Unbelievable. Kyle and Hannah were already on their way out through the lobby, and I was too dejected to do the whole "Call your boss" thing. I followed Kyle and our new daughter out. "Pride! The gays! The damn gays!" I yelled as we walked out into the street, trying to lighten the souring mood.

I pulled out my phone to look up more hotels when Kyle pointed over my shoulder. "Laci, look!" I spun around only to see the glowing green and blue light of the Holiday Inn Express. Damn, did that bitch look inviting.

"It's worth a try," I said. As we walked the quarter block to the Holiday Inn Express, I saw us through the lens of a hotel clerk: two Black girls, one carrying a clear plastic trash bag with food and clothing, the other a few martinis deep, and a white gay guy who was also riding the martini train, all three purporting to be part of the same cohort. It wasn't going to work. People have too many opinions about a crew like ours. So I put on my scammer brain. As soon as we walked into the Holiday Inn Express, I told Hannah to keep her plastic bag out of the eye line of the clerk and slammed my credit card on the desk. "Hi, I'm looking to put up my cousin for the night." I nodded toward Hannah and then stared directly back at the clerk, giving him my best *I've got nothing to hide here, sir.*

My confidence, the cousin con, and my credit card worked—we got a room. Fucking finally. As we walked to the elevators, I noticed a wall of snacks in the lobby. Nothing fancy. Some water, chips, Starbucks. "Do you want something?" I asked Hannah. She shook her head, "No." Of course she didn't want anything; she probably just wanted to get rid of these two drunk idiots infantilizing her and be left alone.

"No, girl, come on," I told her. "We have to get you something."

"Okay," Hannah sighed. She walked over, surveyed the snacks, then took two waters and a Starbucks coffee.

"Great." I grabbed the drinks from her and went to the desk to pay. But when I got to the desk, I noticed a line, and I don't wait in lines. So I just stole the food. The hotel's crappy payment system made me do it! As we got to Hannah's room, Kyle and I hung back. We didn't want to violate her privacy. I knew she wasn't too hot on Kyle being around, so we just kind of lingered there to make sure Hannah was safely inside. As soon as her door shut, Kyle and I unclenched our jaws. We were so relieved that we'd found Hannah a place to stay. Sure, it took us all night, but at least she was safe.

I ordered another Uber (at this point I'm keeping the lights on over there), and we headed back to my apartment for wine—about four hours after we'd initially planned. "That. Was. Crazy," Kyle said as he poured himself a second glass. "Girl," I told him, "I know."

The next morning, I was woken up by a phone call from a number I didn't recognize. When I picked it up, I was surprised to hear a man coming at me HOT.

"Ms. Mosley, this is [I Don't Remember His Name] from the Holiday Inn Express. Are you still in your room?" My stomach sank. *Fuck.* It was too early and I was too tired/ semihungover to spin this, so I just went with the truth. "Full Disclosure: I actually rented that room out to an unhoused woman who was in front of my building . . . Why? Is there a problem?"

I could hear the man scoff on the other line. "Actually, yes, there is. Whoever is in the room you rented is not coming out." Suddenly, the man on the other end of the line put on a father voice and added, "I've gotta tell you, you've put yourself at immense risk. You clearly don't know this person. And because you put your credit card down, it's your name attached to the room and you are now liable for any damages or theft." I winced. *Sorry, Holiday Inn Dad, I was just trying to be a good person.*

"Well, what happens now?" I asked my Holiday Inn Dad.

"Our cleaning service moved on to the next floor since they didn't get an answer. I'm going to try to send someone up there to assess the damage as soon as possible. I'll call back as soon as we get into the room."

I got off the phone with my Holiday Inn Dad and called my husband, Kyle, who was at a diner eating off his hangover. As soon as he answered, I launched into it and told him what his Holiday Inn Father-in-Law had said.

"Kyle, Hannah has barricaded herself in the room. She's not coming out. WHY DIDN'T YOU STOP ME FROM RENTING A ROOM OUT TO A STRANGER?! I am liable!"

"I thought I was helping you do a good thing!"

"I thought I was helping *YOU* do a good thing!"

The conversation proved to be useless. So I hung up to focus on the task at hand, which was to completely and wholly freak the fuck out. *Oh My God I got scammed!!! And now I'm going to owe Visa one Holiday Inn Express!* I do not have "buy a Holiday Inn Express" money!!! At this point, my anxiety had fully kicked in and I was tripping.

I decided the only thing that would help my spiraling was if I took one of my MENTO health walks around the neighborhood. There really was nothing to do but wait until my Holiday Inn Dad gave me a call back to let me know if I was on the hook for an entire midtier hotel in the middle of Hollywood. I made it about half a block before I gave in to my freak-out and called the Holiday Inn Express.

"Hi," I said, putting on my best keeping-shit-together voice, "I'm the idiot that rented a room for a stranger yesterday."

"Oh. Hi, Ms. Mosley. I was just about to call you back. We managed to get back into the room. There was no damage. Your guest is gone. But I have to advise you against doing this again because it opens you up to fraud."

"Okay, great. Bye." I got off the phone as quickly as I could because fuck that guy. He was like all the other motherfuckers who made a bad situation worse by slathering their preconceived notions onto decent human beings trying to get by in this shit world.

I hope Hannah is okay and what Kyle and I did was the right thing to do—even if we didn't go about it in the most graceful manner. Hannah ultimately wasn't a scammer, but most people looked at her like she was. It wasn't just Holiday Inn Dad; it was everyone. Our Uber drivers, people on the street, other hotel workers. I could feel their glares on us, and it didn't feel good. People stereotype the unhoused as criminals who will try to take advantage of you at every turn, when in reality they're just human beings, part of our society, who need a little extra help feeling safe and supported.

I want you to know I didn't tell you this to seem like a fucking hero. I told you this because I've had *a lot* of help in my life and I owe it to the universe to return the favor. This book is about how to spot scams, but it's not about becoming cynical to the world. It's not about turning away from an opportunity to pay it forward.

Jasmine may have scammed me out of my mama's purse change, but it didn't harden my heart. Sometimes in life you get scammed by a new friend and you owe your mama one Black History essay; other times you help out a new friend and you *don't* owe Chase Visa one Holiday Inn Express! The point is: everything is a scam, but not *everyone* is a scammer. In our fucked-up world with its unfair rules, it's impossible not to encounter scammy things; they're in the water. But in order to be a true-blue scammer, you have to intentionally enter a relationship with the goal of hurting another person, and not all people are out there to hurt you. Some might do it on accident, but they don't mean it. I just want y'all to know that. Be vigilant, but don't close yourself off from the world and the people in it.

Body Scams

A huge crux of the scam that *is* capitalism is creating a need where there is none. I find that the biggest extorter of this crux is THE ENTIRE BEAUTY INDUSTRY. The beauty industry makes us constantly insecure about the bodies God gave us because that's how they earn that easy living: selling trendy diets, fat camps, weight loss pills, buccal fat surgery (lol), creams, dyes, highlighters, lifters, cinchers, tapes, corsets—there's not enough room in this damn book to list all the grifty ways cosmetics are conning us.

Now, it's easy for me to sit here on my throne in Los Angeles—a city that's keeping the entire Botox industry afloat—and tell you to ignore all of the nonsense that magazines, commercials, television, and movies have been shoving down our throats for the past sixty-three million years. Even when dinosaurs were roaming the earth, you know they were like, "Oh girl, your skin's looking a little lizardy. Here, try this anemone cream; it'll take those damn years off." It's hard for me to really speak passionately for or against body positivity because I'm part of an industry that uses bodies as tools to sell; whether it's a story, a lifestyle, or—sigh—some ad space. Unfortunately, using my appearance to sell stuff is how I get to make the art that I want to make.

What I can offer you is a truthful snapshot of what it's like to be an actor in the entertainment industry in all its unfiltered, nasty glory. I always knew that my desire to be a performer would be linked to the industry's desire to put traditionally praised bodies on-screen. As a dark-skinned Black woman, I also knew that I'd be going into this fucking circus with the cards stacked against me.

When I was young, I thought I had to make my body as small as possible so I could fit on that crowded stage. In high school, I was really athletic thanks to all the sports I joined to appease my mom enough to let me out of the house. I had the thick, muscular body of a girl who could spike a volleyball and run the 100 meter dash, long jump, triple jump, and a 4-by-100 meter relay. My high school years were bursting with endless opportunities to be active, to move, to live a balanced life of academics, athletics, and the arts.

When I got to college at Pitt, and a little bit closer to my dream of moving to Los Angeles, I took all my top-of-the-class studious energy and applied it to getting the perfect LA body. I was working out all the time and doing whatever Le Diet Trend of the month was. One summer, when I was working as a college tour guide—I mean, *Pathfinder*—I really fucked up my metabolism trying to prepare for *Dream Girls*, a movie that had already been out for five years and I had absolutely zero chance of being retroactively cast in. At the time, I was working these things called "Programs," which basically meant you had to scrape your hungover ass up at 6 a.m. to trick prospective kids into going to Pitt by lovebombing them. When the students eventually got accepted and moved into the dorms . . . you'd run back toward your real friends and forget they ever existed.

Our days as Pathfinders were intense. We'd get up at the ass-crack of dawn to do a Welcome Breakfast at our dining hall, featuring the stalest pastries you ever did see, then we'd chat with the parents of the prospective students who would sell up their kids like they were used cars on Craigslist. After that there was a walking tour through the campus, and then a breakout panel where we'd discuss majors. But wait, there's more: after being served stale, unappetizing food *again*, followed by a bus tour of campus and the city (my favorite part of the day because Pitt was dumb enough to provide me with a microphone and a speaker), there would be dinner and even more evening activities. It was a full fucking day, but I loved it.

My first summer as a Pathfinder was also the same time I found out about the Beyoncé Diet, which is technically called the Master Cleanse, but since that sounds like some sort of Nazi propaganda, we're going to stick to the Beyoncé Diet. Back in 2006, Beyoncé was still giving interviews (before she stopped talking to us all), and she started telling every Tom, Dick, and Oprah about the special lemon-cayenne-water diet she used to "prepare" for her role in *Dream Girls*. Even though the diet was invented in the 1980s, it didn't really pop off until Beyoncé shone her light on the cause. Ever since then, like allergies, it comes back seasonally to fuck a bunch of bitches up. Even now, today, if you google "Beyoncé Diet," I promise you an article published within the last six months will fill your feed.

I loved Beyoncé (still do), and I wanted to be just like her. Okay, yes, now you have the likes of the Kardashians selling skinny lollipops and starvation gummy bears everywhere you look, but back then I didn't know these celebrities were hawking snake oil. I thought it was all cute tips for how to prepare for roles. If an actor as talented and beautiful as Beyoncé was eating lemons to act, I was like, start squeezin' baby. Gimme those lemons, life!

I couldn't spend like a celebrity. I couldn't dress like a celebrity. I couldn't work like a celebrity. But I sure as hell could eat like one. Like so many other Black girls and wannabe-Black girls that summer, I ran my ass over to Giant Eagle and loaded up the cart with lemons, cayenne, and maple syrup. Y'all, I came home and made so much of that fucking lemon water that my little tiny college freezer was busting out of her suit.

At the time, I didn't know you could have a bad relationship with food, because I didn't know you could *be* in a relationship with food. My friends were always making comments like, "Laci, we never see you eat!" My broken little brain thought it was a compliment. Look at me, not eating. Such restraint! The diet of my idols! I'm ready for the red carpet! All summer, I'd wake up early, give my tours, sip my lemon water, work out, then do it all again the next day. Time dragged on. It started getting hotter; I started to get smaller; but I also started to get weaker.

Then, on one of the hottest days of the year, I was nursing my lemon water, walking backward while recounting the history of Pitt, when my vision began to blur. I took a deep breath, shook it off, and powered through the rest of the tour. But during lunchtime my friend and fellow Pathfinder Marshall started looking at me funny. I was used to Marshall looking at me funny because he was this hilarious Jewish dude whose love language was roasting people. But this time he wasn't laughing.

"Laci," Marshall said, touching my arm, his face serious for the first time ever, "you're swaying."

"Oh, yeah, I'm just a little dizzy because I'm on the Beyoncé Diet," I responded.

"The what?"

"The Beyoncé Diet."

Explaining, out loud, the details of the lemon-water diet and why I was on it made me realize how ridiculous it sounded. Based on Marshall's startled and perplexed reaction, I immediately realized that this was *not* the right way to get smaller.

I wish I could tell you this was the moment I learned that wanting to be smaller in the first place was a scam, that after that moment I knew I should not waste my time becoming a Thin Hollywood Model Baby—that I look perfectly fine at whatever size I am! But anyone with a body knows that's not how this shit works. Especially in the entertainment industry, where your body is a product—we *are* objects. We are little dolls you set up in the way you want. If your doll is too tall or too short, too big or too medium (no such thing as too small in Hollywood!), then you won't get to work or keep working. That's exactly why I fell into the next scam. Yes, me. This one is a con that's been plaguing your girl.

OH, NO, NO, NO-ZEMPICCCC.

Hollywood is the reason that half the world knows about Ozempic, and if you don't know about Ozempic, wheeew . . . you're about to. All diet culture is a scam, but Ozempic is a *real* racket right now. Basically, Ozempic is a drug used to treat Type 2 diabetes, and some genius figured out that this drug also makes you lose weight. Now that shit is flying off the shelves like hotcakes. Like there are shortages of this diabetes drug for the people who actually need it because half the entertainment industry is on it.

I first heard of Ozempic while sitting in the makeup chair. The lovely makeup artist was plugging up my pores with creams and powders and all sorts of different shit when she said, "Have you heard of this new skinny shot?" She proceeded to tell me about a clinic hidden deep in the heart of Beverly Hills that was shooting up all the Hollywood celebs with this skinny-making diabetes medicine. I couldn't believe what I was hearing. How stupid do you have to be to take a drug designed to regulate insulin secretion to try to look good? I made an appointment as soon as I got home.

According to the makeup artist, getting a shot was as easy as calling the clinic and setting up an appointment. I was too nervous to do it myself, so I made my highly talented, extremely capable assistant, Emily, do it. Emily, who has most likely never purchased any sort of drugs in her entire life, let alone shady-ass skinny drugs, asked me what to tell the clinic when they asked what the appointment was for. "Just tell them it's for the weight loss."

Emily responded, "They don't have a box to check for that . . . What exactly are you looking for?"

I didn't want my organized queen to know I was copping skinny shots, so I said again, but slower, "Just tell them it's for weight loss. They'll know what that means."

I figured they'd know what that means because it's, uh, extremely clear what that means.

Emily made the appointment and emailed me the calendar confirmation—and then the guilt set in. I'd just done a podcast talking about how unethical it is to steal diabetes drugs from people (a thing I deeply believe), and I began to feel like a hypocrite (a thing I deeply was being). "What are you doing?!" my brain kept screaming, "YOU DON'T HAVE DIABETES!" Even though Ozempic is FDA approved for weight loss—and we know *they're* reliable as fuck 👀—this is all so new. Does anyone *really* know what happens when you take diabetes shots for weight loss? Ugh. I was being so dumb. Shortly after I asked her to make it, I texted Emily to cancel the appointment.

But here's the thing. This was all unfolding a little before my birthday, which is the Fourth of July. I don't think I'm surprising anyone here when I say that I'm a birthday diva. I like to throw enormous bangers and call it the Fourth of JuLaci. I go big. And in thinking about my birthday, I realized that it'd be a crime not to wear a bikini. What with climate change making it snow in LA, who knows how many bikini birthdays I have left? It'd be straight-up unfair to keep the people from seeing my ass in a G-string. As soon as I canceled that appointment, I began to think about how much better I'd look with that Ozempic body. So, a few weeks later, I asked Emily to rebook my appointment. "Of course," came her response. I could feel the "bitches be crazy" energy vibrating from the phone.

When Emily rescheduled the appointment, I got a confirmation email in which I found out each shot is $1,000. A thousand dollars, y'all. For one shot. And you need to take Ozempic once a week for three months, take a break, and then start the process again with a higher dosage. I think. That's how little attention I was paying to the details. All you need to know is that it's expensive as hell. I have money, but not a-thousand-dollars-a-shot money. "GIRL," my brain screamed even louder, "STOP ACTING LIKE YOU HAVE DIABETES!" I sighed and pulled up Emily's number again: "Can you cancel the appointment?" I put my phone away and prayed that Emily wouldn't respond with a resignation letter.

All this happened just last month. I am living proof that the actors are not alright. Yes, I'm more healed than when I was sipping on lemon water, getting all dizzy in the quad, but I'm not fully healed. It's all a process. Loving yourself is a choice every day. Some days, I make my assistant schedule me a diabetes-skinny-shot appointment. Other days, I ask her to cancel the exact same appointment. (Please don't quit, Emily.) All we can do is try our best to have more of the brain-yelly days and fewer of the do-insane-things-to-change-your-body days.

YASSIFICATION OF STARVATION

Ozempic isn't the only body-image fuckery I've fallen prey to. Have you ever worn Spanx? What about two pairs? What about three pairs under a faja full body suit? I have. I have rearranged my organs to be allowed onto the red carpet. You think I came up with these ideas on my own? No. Did I enthusiastically shove my intestines into my spine like I was warmly encouraged to do? Hell-the-fuck-yes. Again, I'm not complaining. You ask me to be babyGap sample size? Sure! You want me to squeeze into a thimble for the premiere? Great! You need me to wear this promise ring as a belt? Okay!

I remember being at a party, chatting up another actor who was telling me some "preparing for a role" tips she's learned over the years, and one of them was eating nothing but steamed broccoli and boiled chicken. "If you get hungry," she told me between sips of her vodka soda, "you can have a spoon of almond butter to hold you over." I *thanked* her for letting me know. Gave her an unironic, "Thanks for the tip, girl!" We are starving ourselves to get work. No matter how much the beauty industry celebrates bodies of all shapes and sizes (so that they can sell you an $80 pair of leggings with "tummy control" built in), Hollywood continues to shove the thinnest, most sickly looking people on camera. Sure, a thicc-bootied baddy will sneak in every now and then, but it's very rare, and when it does happen, the amount of executive back-patting will sprain a wrist or two.

The worst part is that we're out here trying to change societal perspectives through marketing campaigns that are never going to work. *That's* the scam of it all. As long as someone's trying to sell you something, whether it's leggings, fiber powder, a movie, a diet pill, or a lifestyle, they're always going to need to create a desire, a want, a *need*. We're all cogs in the machine, forced to keep the capitalism monster fed, but what the shortsighted money people don't realize is that it's taking a toll on us all.

I struggle with depression, and because of this, sometimes I gain a little weight. Like 100 percent of people with depression, I still have to work, maybe even more so, so that I can get the medication I need to function normally. I can't shrug away when my body changes; there is an entire team of people monitoring my size because their job depends on it. There is paperwork with my measurements floating around various offices in Los Angeles.

Because of this, it's hard to ignore changes with my body when I have fittings.

During fittings, the wardrobe department wraps measuring tape around the "smallest" parts of my body, putting clothing on, ripping clothing off, giving off hmms of surprise when something doesn't fit or looks too tight. One time, I hadn't even realized I'd gained weight. I just walked onto set one day and all of a sudden there were no crop tops in my wardrobe and all my shirts were replaced with unflattering pillowcases . . . no drip to be had anywhere. Wardrobe was like, "Here, Laci! We pulled this gorgeous tarp for you! Isn't it beautiful? Try it on, it's gonna look so cute on your curves."

These annoying, teeny microaggressions stick with you. And if it's like this for me, I can't imagine what it's like for my plus-size babes out here because every number you go up over a size 4 in Hollywood increases the casual disgust you're exposed to on a daily basis. It's ugly. It's nasty. I do not participate in the disgusting habits, but I struggle to push back against those who do. When you do what I've done to get yourself onstage, you're not about to start setting fires the second you get inside the building.

Plus, I'd prepared myself for the industry to be like this. Hollywood is living up to my lowest expectations. Thanks, girl! Everyone outside and inside Hollywood knows how toxic the environment is. You have to shake hands with the devil and sacrifice your physical form, for a shot at your dreams. It's not right and I hope it changes, but I really don't know how.

I remember this one night, I was lying in bed and I felt like shit. I was burning up but also somehow cold. I thought I was going to sweat my damn eyebrows off. Every time I moved, I felt like I'd been filet-o-fished. I couldn't even move myself for a glass of water. I was going on day two of being unable to get out of bed. I was crawling on my hands and knees—not even in the sexy stripper way, but in the save-me-Jesus kind of way.

Now, I'd rather die than ask for help, but on this night, it seemed like the dying might actually happen. And I was like, *Uh-oh, what if a bitch has appendicitis?* So I called my best friend in the whole wide world, my mom—you know, to say goodbye and whatnot. *I had a good run, but this is it. At least I'm going to die hot.* When I told my mom I was dying, all she said was: "Laci, don't be stupid. Call an ambulance."

I am an obedient person and I typically do everything my mom tells me to do, but even in my fever-pain delirium, I knew there was no way I was about to call a thousands-of-dollars Uber. I would just call a tens-of-dollars Uber and hope that I didn't die in a stranger's car. But when I texted my mom the plan, she was not. having. it. So after a delicate but effective back-and-forth, we both settled on me calling a friend for a favor. The thought of someone seeing me *that* down bad caused me even more pain than I was already physically in.

The only person I could think to call was Mary. A little something about Mary: she is one of the daintiest, littlest white women ever. We met doing make-'em-ups at the Upright Citizens Brigade. And when I first met Mary, I did not trust her at all. She seemed too nice. Like, what are you really about? What's the catch? I kept it light and distant with her for a long time. But here's the thing about Mary: she is the fucking best human being. It was impossible to avoid her light. One time, apropos of nothing, Mary brought me melatonin chocolates and a lavender candle. Just because. She didn't want anything in return aside from my friendship. My guard began to drop with each sweet, chocolaty bite. *Okay, Mary*, I thought, *you can be my white girlfriend.* That was six years ago, and we've been close friends ever since.

Mary is exactly the kind of friend you want by your side when shit goes down. I'd have zero problems dying in her car. So, when I finally realized that my reluctance to ask for help wasn't worth dying over, I called Mary.

"Hiii!" came her chipper-Disney-princess voice.

"Hey, girl, what you doin'?" I asked, trying to sound cool, calm, and not dying.

"Not much, just finished dinner, watching TV. You?"

"Cool. Do you know if you have time to drive me to the hospital?"

Mary was over within minutes, delicately loading my sweaty, decaying body into her car. Once we got to the hospital—during COVID—it was clear that I wasn't dying hard enough to get into the actual ER. So they made me sit in the waiting room and die a little more before they'd admit me. I thought it was going to be like *Grey's Anatomy*, where they would pop me on one of those wheely carts and scream *CCs of this, CCs of that* over my head before saving my life. But nuh-uh. It was paperwork as far as the eye could see.

Before I could protest, Mary plopped right down into one of those uncomfortable plastic seats. I *told* her she should go home, that it was going to be a long night, and she said, "No." Then I *asked* her to go home, because it was going to be a long night, and she said, "No." Then I *begged* her to go home, because of the whole long night thing, and still, she said, "No." Even though Mary had work in the morning and it was in the middle of a terrifying pandemic where hospitals felt like wartime (shout out to the health care girlies), Mary just sank further and further into the chair. She wasn't gonna leave me there alone. Not everyone gets to have a Mary in their life, but I'm lucky to have one in mine.

I very slowly, painfully took a seat next to her and waited. The first hour, it was almost fun. The emergency waiting room of a hospital in Los Angeles, California, has a lot of world-class people-watching. The second hour, Mary and I realized that people who had the pain (and money) to come by ambulance were getting the true *Grey's Anatomy* CCs-yelling treatment. Every twenty minutes or so, the big metal double doors would swing open and some fine-looking EMTs would rush in with a body taped to a stretcher. They'd make a big show, before turning the corner and disappearing through another set of double doors right next to where Mary and I were sitting. Every time another patient was wheeled into the emergency room, right under our noses, I kept getting angrier and angrier that I didn't pay the $50 million for the *Grey's Anatomy* treatment.

The third hour, I finally got called up to the desk, and you would've thought I was on the fucking *Price Is Right*. Mary and I grabbed hands and I cheered through my searing pain. *Ooooh, I'm going to win myself a diagnosis, Drew!* But they just wanted to check my vitals to make sure I was still dying at a manageable pace. I was, so they sent me back to my uncomfortable plastic seat. I told Mary we would probably better off if she dropped me on the curb and I called an ambulance. That 50k Uber was a VIP ticket to the ER. The fourth hour, those big metal doors swung open, and the fine-ass EMTs burst in with a woman on a stretcher, but right as I was thinking how lucky this ambulance-riding bitch was, it all went sideways . . . literally. Instead of turning the corner and disappearing through the set of double doors next us, the EMTs took the left too fast and the woman . . . TUMBLED OUT OF THE STRETCHER LIKE A COOKIE OFF A HOT TIN PAN.

I don't know if she wasn't taped down properly or what. All I know is that I'll never forget the slapsticky horror of watching her body tumble out the stretcher and roll onto the floor. I was like, *Damn, this woman paid one hundred bazillion dollars to get the* Grey's Anatomy *CCs-yelling treatment, and they're tossing her around like a sack o' potatoes.* Look y'all, yes it was horrendous, but it was also the funniest shit I'd ever seen in my entire life. I was gagging. For a second, I thought I was going to cough up my appendix right then and there. Dying laughing is a good way to go if you can

manage it. Mary and I are forever bonded because **absur-
dity bonds are stronger than
trauma bonds**. It almost made
sitting in the ER until 1 a.m.
during a society-shattering
pandemic worth it.

Eventually, I got in to see
the ER doctor and was able to
send Mary home so she could

SCAM LIFE LESSON
Absurdity bonds are stronger than trauma bonds.

get some sleep before work. Turns out, I had a fibroid
the size of "a cantaloupe" and the fibroid had become
necrotic. COOL! The ER doctor said I'd need to schedule
a C-section-like surgery with my gyno immediately, and
I was like, "Hol up. Wait a minute, doc." Here's the thing
about my gyno: He's a perfectly nice man, but he is old as
time. He learned how to do C-sections in 1904 when they
sliced up a bitch like she was discount deli ham at Kroger.
Considering every inch of my body belongs to the entertainment industry, I wasn't very into the whole emergency surgery thing. But no matter how much I begged,
bartered, and refused . . . the surgery had to happen. I had
fucking fruit growing in my uterus.

I decided that if I was going to get cut, I'd better be cut
cute. Luckily, my gyno knew the guy who does the hottest, trendiest mommy cuts in all of Los Angeles. See? I
told you shit is fucked up here. I wasn't the first vain bitch
to be like, gimme that cute surgery, bruh. Only water
stitches and laparoscopic cuts for your girl Laci.

Look, I need to pause here to say, I know y'all. I know. This sounds bad because it is bad. There's nothing wrong with a little C-section scar. I'M A C-SECTION BABY! If anything, having a C-section scar would bring me closer to my idol: my mom. Sure, I wouldn't have a baby from it, but I could rock the battle wounds just the same. But also . . . Hollywood, remember? Casting directors aren't going to take the time to unpack why my belly has a battle wound . . . they're just going to yell *next* and bring in some unmarked spoils.

To make matters worse, right as I was getting out of the hospital, I checked my phone only to see that at some point during my ER stint, I'd booked a recurring role on *Lopez vs. Lopez.* So I needed that cute surgery ASAP. I saw the specialist on a Wednesday; he booked me for surgery by Friday. Before I went under, he mentioned that there was a chance the fibroid would be too large to remove laparoscopically; if that was the case, they'd have to cut me open. To which I said, "Nah, that ain't it." Of course, he shrugged and ignored me because that's what doctors do: ignore fine-looking Black ladies. He said that I'd either wake up with little laparoscopic incisions that would eventually disappear or a C-section scar that'd be hidden under my bikini line—but either way he wasn't about to put me under twice to remove a life-threatening fibroid. *Okay, whatever. You're the specialist.* I took a deep breath, signed some paperwork saying I wouldn't sue if I died, prayed to Jesus and my mom that I wouldn't get cut up bad, and went under. I woke up with the C-section scar.

Of course, it was fine. The scar is tiny in the grand scheme of things, and no one really knows about it or sees it but, you know, they have me doing all kinds of things for auditions and sometimes it comes up. Just a few months ago, I had to put myself on tape for a role as a stripper. I knew I wouldn't get naked for the role because these aren't Halle Berry *Monster's Ball* titties, but there was a chance you'd see my scar. Still, the role was for a dancer on *P-Valley*, which is an excellent show, and I really wanted the part. So I set up my little iPhone and ring light situation and did my best. I put on "Bitch From Da Souf (South)" by Latto and began twerking for the camera, doing jump splits, making my fiercest, sexiest stripper eye contact.

Before sending the tape in, I sent it to my cousins, because Black people are hella honest and I wanted to make sure I didn't look like a complete idiot. And, yup, I'm pretty sure my cousins are *still* laughing about it to this very day. My one cousin said, "Why are you dancing like it's a threat?" But at least they didn't notice the scar.

Shortly after that audition, I was watching *Bust Down* on Peacock, a hilarious show with an incredible cast, when out of nowhere they had a joke that said: "It was a bad surprise, like a stripper with a C-section scar." That joke was a dagger through my heart. I could feel my abs tense around my "bad surprise." Don't get me wrong—it's a well-written joke. But it also hurts my soul.

Until we stop talking about bodies completely, there's just no escaping it. And I'm not really sure if our culture is capable of not talking about bodies. Bodies are one of the only universal things all humans have in common, and that's why we're always going to be obsessing about our own and others'. Considering everything I've seen, everything I've been through, and everything I've learned, I now know that my relationship with my body is something I'll need to work on every day for the rest of my life. People—and especially the wellness industry—will always try to come at you and damage your relationship with your body; the key is to be prepared for it and ready to reprogram the narrative you're building in your head.

I don't think I'll ever shake the feeling that my body is constantly and consistently being scrutinized. I don't know if any actor in Los Angeles can ever truly get right with themselves. But I *have* gotten better. I no longer starve myself like I did in college because that's stupid as fuck and totally bad for your health. I stopped working out like a maniac and mostly just do enough to keep my endorphins up. But I have to coach myself out of negative thinking and bad behavior every single day. I also have to monitor my social media consumption—anywhere human bodies are showcased is a place you have to be extra fastidious about checking in on your reactions and how you're being affected.

Like most young women who want to feel pretty and praised, I've gotten too lit editing a pic or two ... The whole-ass internet has gone so overboard with the filters that it feels like we're at a collective rock bottom. I've started posting raw photos because we just have to collectively stop using filters. We have to protect our mental health. We have to fix the imagery that little girls are see-ing. Being in Hollywood, under the scrutiny of the public eye, has exacerbated all my jacked-up body-image issues, but at the same time, it has provided a fail-safe, too. I'm on fucking TV, which means I can't use filters to change what my body and face look like online because people are going to know that it's not me. Look at Khloé Kardashian pinching in her waist until

SCAM LIFE LESSON

Don't let anyone trick you into thinking you're not hot enough.

the walls behind her go zigzaggy. Folks are on her ass. The internet knows. Girl, Khloé, quit it with the zigzaggy walls. You be you!

The internet is the worst place in the world, but I'll give it one thing: it demands authenticity. When people online find out you're doing something shady, they love bringing it out into the timeline. Maybe my motivations for putting my real ass out online are vain, but let me remind you: as a professional actor in Hollywood, it's all about appearances, honey. I'm just learning to be cool with my appearance regardless of what's trendy or what a casting agent says looks good on camera.

The moral of this chapter, y'all, is: **don't let anyone trick you into thinking you're not hot enough**. Anyone who is trying to minimize you is looking to maximize themselves in some way. And while we're at it, don't trust what any of the actors or media personalities say, because we're using your attention to get money. No one cares about wellness or health; they just care about getting that dollar. There will always be these nasty little moments peppered throughout our lives that confirm our greatest fears about ourselves. When it comes to your body, the way you look, there's only so much you can do to change it, but what's easier to change is your mind, your perspective.

Like I said, I'm not about to be this conventionally attractive actress who has trainers and nutritionists telling YOU how to achieve your greatest self. I have a team of professionals helping me look good, and I *still* have my bad days. All I'm here to say is ignore it all. Ignore what Hollywood says, what your skinny friends have told you, what your fat friends have told you, what your brain has told you, what *I* have told you, and do what makes you feel good. That's the way you outscam the body scammers. Amen. X

Familial Scams

My family is the best. It's been nothing but love and support for Laci and her wild dreams. Since my family is so close, there's no way in hell I'd put our business in this chapter. So you'll never know about our hustles, because **the true mark of a skilled Scam Goddess is knowing when to keep your damn mouth shut**.

SCAM LIFE LESSON

The true mark of a skilled Scam Goddess is knowing when to keep your damn mouth shut.

There's basically nothing my family won't do for each other, so when it comes to familial scams, I understand why they happen. Regardless of what your nuclear, chosen, or generally fucked-up crew is like, family comes with a feeling of loyalty for a lot of us. I get it, these are people you owe your LIFE to whether you want to or not. There are rarely any boundaries. Even if you figure out how the hell to create some, they're never enforced. Parents *made you* to have a smaller, weaker version of themselves to boss around forever and ever. These complicated interlaced dynamics are why you often see families behaving badly *together*. Like the family I'm about to tell you about.

KEEPING UP WITH THE JOHNSES

When researching the best family of fraudsters to dig into for this chapter, I was temped to go Trump or Kardashian, because those are two iconic, blue-blooded American scamilies right there. But to be honest, I'm kind of tired of both, and there aren't enough trees in the world to print enough pages to dig into exactly all of the nuanced ways these families are tricking people out of their hard-earned money, time, attention, and energy. So I'm gonna instead direct your attention to John and JonAtina Barksdale (yes, his name is John and her name is JonAtina . . . of all the names to double up on . . .), a brother-sister duo accused of scamming 20,000 investors out of $124 million. Which honestly sounds exhausting, TBH.

There's not much information about John or JonAtina on the web, other than the fact that they ran a company together called iAM Marketing. Direct branding, I like it. According to their website—which is still somehow miraculously live at the time of this writing, despite the fact that the Barksdales have the Securities and Exchange Commission breathing down their backs—they offer "high performance marketing for the blockchain and cryptocurrency industry." Cool, so some type of nonsense. This website was definitely giving me ChatGPT Is Your Creative Director vibes. There's no soul, just a bunch of business jargon that probably sounds good to people with money to waste.

JonAtina is listed as the founder of the company, and John is listed as the chairman. Honestly, unless it's like a mom-and-pop, I am always going to assume any business—especially one with lots of money involved—run by family members is a scam.

Apparently, I am not the only one who feels this way because in 2022 the SEC charged the siblings with conspiracy and securities and wire fraud. According to the SEC, the two were basically running a crypto multilevel marketing scheme. Ahhh, MLMs, the basic bitch of the scam world. Even though JonAtina was running iAM Marketing, it was John's other firm, Ormeus Global S.A., which he also coran with JonAtina, that was the problem child in the scamily.

According to the U.S. Attorney's Office (ooooh, you're in trouble now, John-Jon), the siblings were allegedly lying to investors about the profitability of Ormeus Coin's mining assets. After raising millions upon millions of dollars from investors, the two were seen on social media traveling the world with their other six siblings and mom. Reporters found the Barksdales' names on multiple properties throughout the United States, and on John's Facebook page, he said he had traveled to sixty-one countries in three years and was shooting for one hundred in five. Clearly the two were too busy spending their investors' coin to, you know, actually invest any of it.

SCAM LIFE LESSON
If anyone tells you you're going to get rich quick ... RUN.

Here's another hot tip for you: if anyone in the cryptocurrency world tells you you're gonna get rich quick, RUN. Fuck, man, **if anyone tells you you're going to get rich quick ... RUN**. Pretty quickly after starting the business, the two raised millions of dollars from thousands of investors by selling them subscription packages to their crypto MLM and promising a huge return on investment. The two used other traditional scammer tactics, too: inflating their wealth through razzle-dazzle-'em lies and fake social media posts—your traditional lazy lying fare. In a statement to journalists, Melissa Hodgman, associate director of the SEC enforcement division, called the Barksdales "modern-day snake-oil salesmen." At least snake oil is a tangible good. Bad crypto is just made-up ones and zeros.

Last I read, the Barksdales owed the government *a lot* of money, like over $100 million a lot. But other than that, there hasn't been any follow-up on the two. JonAtina is still kicking it on Instagram, working out, posting meaningless content that encourages you to "lose the poverty mentality" because then "everything is free," and John is nowhere to be seen. I, personally, think it's cute the two stole millions upon millions of dollars and got to traverse the world with their family with it. But then again, I know better than to trust a brother-sister duo promising to make me incredibly rich.

ON SET WITH THE SCHEMIN' SCAMERETTE

After I got *Florida Girls*, I was finally getting attention from agents and reps because there was finally a way for them to make money off me. I immediately started getting opportunities to audition for more things, and one of those things was a horror-comedy movie. Yes, horror-comedy. It's a perfect union. Both genres are all about timing and jacking up your adrenaline. The movie was being produced by a famous sibling duo known for their corner on the indie comedy market. Okay, before you get on me about the whole not-trusting-the-nepo-network thing, it's impossible to avoid nepotism in Hollywood. And besides, I already told you: I don't take my own advice.

The director of this film, who I'll call Chelsea, was also the writer and star. Yas to women in filmmaking. You go, Chelsea. She was doing everything, honey. Love to see it! I could *not* think of something more fun than shooting a horror-comedy movie produced by people I respected and created by a badass forging her own path in the industry. Needless to say, I crushed the audition because I'm good at what I do, and I got the part. I was so excited. I'd only done one tiny movie you've never heard of (and had my moment with Ice-T), and I knew this could be my opportunity to level up. As soon as I got offered the part, I was all, "Yes, yes! A million times yes." But my reps were tepid, mostly because it was an incredibly small budget. Reps do not get out of bed unless *you* make six figures on a project. They told me to hold off on accepting until I saw who else would get attached. Fine. Whatever. I waited.

A few weeks, or months, later (What is time? Who cares.), I found out that Milana Vayntrub, Tig Notaro, Ally Beardsley, and another successful comedic actress friend of mine who I'll call Lisa Larsen would all be in the movie. Bet. Flawless lineup. I'm about to be shooting this movie with my crew. This *is* my *Girls Trip*. Scoot over Tiffany Haddish, I'm about to be ready too. My reps agreed: with this group of heavy hitters, this movie was a must-do.

Before I'd even had the chance to fully unpack my bags from filming *Florida Girls* in Georgia, I was already making plans to spend a month in a big coastal city. (Yes, movie-shooting schedules are insanely fast because time is money, bb.) All I knew about this city was what I'd seen on TV. Nothing else. But I was thrilled. It felt like all my acting dreams were coming true. I was getting paid good money to stunt on camera and travel the globe. My unquenchable curiosity about the world was *finally* paying off.

I was the first actor to arrive at the airport. When I got off the plane, a driver with my last name on a sign was waiting for me at the exit and everything. He grabbed my bags and led me to a Cadillac SUV courtesy of production. It was the most "I'm a Hollywood actor" shit ever. Not going to lie, it was bomb. I felt cool. I felt powerful. I felt like I'd finally arrived.

The driver took me to my hotel, where I had a wardrobe fitting. Wardrobe fittings can be a nightmare, as you know, with people prodding, poking, and openly discussing your body, but this one wasn't. It was chill with a nice, bubbly, excited crew. The tone for our shoot was being set, and I liked the tempo. The hotel was cute, too. I was surprised. My reps made it seem like this was a real indie-indie movie with no budget, but looking around I was like, okay maybe production does have some coin here. As quickly as they came, wardrobe disappeared, and I spent the evening studying my lines for the next day, snapping selfies with the flattering hotel lighting.

The next day, our first day of filming, I was picked up and whisked away to set, which I quickly realized was the director/writer/star's parents' home in the city (not to be confused with their other house on a nearby island, which we'll get to in a sec). It was a nice-ass house, too. They had all sorts of worldly possessions. Chelsea's parents' home is the first place I ever tried one of those Japanese toilets. The seat was heated, and they had the little thing that shot water up my booty hole. No wonder rich people don't shower! They just shoot water up into their booty hole and leave the rest to God. This house was so nice that they had a dock that went right into the water with a boat ready to go so when the apocalypse comes, they'll just hop right in and float out to sea. Being rich is the shit.

While shooting at someone's family home isn't the most typical thing, crazier favors have been pulled to get a movie made. I think that's what people don't realize: exactly *how many* favors go into making a movie. And if that movie is an indie movie, then the favors get multiplied by a trillion. You literally have directors calling grandma and asking for an advance on their birthday money. It was not at all strange that this whole family was using all the resources they had to make sure Chelsea's production would run smoothly.

At Chelsea's parents' home, the atmosphere was electric—everyone was as excited, if not more so, as I was to be there. Look, the scenery wasn't giving me Steven Spielberg Star Waggons trailers and explosions—it was clear this was going to be a scrappy handheld affair—but the vibe checked all the boxes. There were production assistants milling around, a makeup department, a wardrobe department, a crafty table—legit *teams* of people dedicated to bringing this story to life. And this story was worth bringing to life. The script was actually good. (Not always the case on small-budget features, or honestly, big-budget ones either.) It was about a bachelorette-party retreat for a woman (Chelsea) who was worried she'd said yes to the wrong man. During their girls' trip weird things keep happening as her friends begin getting plucked off one by one. Standard horror-comedy, so you can probably predict how it plays out. But the jokes were fire. The scenes were fun. The pacing was all there. It was no wonder this famous sibling duo had signed on to produce this movie (and by "produce" this movie, I mean lend their names to the marketing materials).

When I met Chelsea, I was a little surprised to see her in person. She . . . just . . . didn't . . . look like the character I'd envisioned in the script. For one, our characters were meant to be the same age, and Chelsea was a good ten years older than me and looked it. My character was about twenty-four or twenty-five years old, and I'm Black, so I have the skin and complexion of an infant. Chelsea's character was about twenty-four or twenty-five years old, and Chelsea was a thirty-six-year-old white woman, who had the skin and complexion of, well, a thirty-six-year-old white woman. No hate, just facts is facts. We really didn't look the same age. But look, homie worked her ass off to get this movie made on her terms and Hollywood is ageist as fuck, so I didn't think twice about it. Then, Chelsea introduced me to her director of photography, aka the one responsible for filming the whole damn thing, Tim (not his real name). It turns out Tim was not only the DP, but he was also Chelsea's fiancé. Wow, curious. We were filming a movie about a woman engaged to the wrong man, and the woman who wrote and was starring in the movie was engaged to DP Tim. *Pulls at collar.* Well, ah, hopefully this isn't an art-imitating-life situation. I'm telling y'all, her mama was catering; the whole family was roped into the thing; so it didn't feel *that* weird that her husband-to-be was helping her tell the story of an engagement gone wrong.

But on our first day of shooting, the weirdness kept piling up. For one, her dad, Phil, was very much present on set and very much eccentric. He immediately began talking Ska music with me, a Black girl from Texas. Even though I had no idea what he was saying, I was intrigued. Phun Phact: Phil was the first Phishhead I ever met in real life. Sure, yes, it's a little distracting to try to do your job when your boss's dad is standing off frame staring at you, but honestly? I found it kind of cute. Like, I'm close with Mama too. I'd love to have her around to see me do my thingies. It was nice to see Chelsea getting so much support in an industry that notoriously treats women like disposable diapers.

The shoot schedule for the first day was intense. We didn't have a lot of time to get all the footage needed, so the pressure was on. *Don't fuck this up, Laci*, I kept telling myself. *Do not slow down production.* Our first scene took place in a car, which might seem simple enough, but is actually extremely tricky to capture because you need the right camera angles to see both actors, you can't get glare from the windshield, and you have to be mic'd in a way that people can hear you but the microphone can't be seen. Another complication was there was only *one* camera and no little monitor to watch playback (i.e., what the director watches to see if the scene turned out the way she wants). This meant that if Chelsea wanted to watch a scene she was acting in, she'd have to get out of the car, have Tim rewind the scene he'd just filmed, check to see if it was done to her liking, then get back in the car—making sure she sits and is lit in a way that matches the previous scenes shot—and continue or reshoot. It's a lot. There was no way, with our schedule and the sun, that Chelsea would be able to watch playback on every scene. So she'd have to direct on vibes like they did in the 1940s, "Cut! We have it, moving on." I'd never seen a director direct on vibes before, and I was here for it, literally in the front seat.

Chelsea called "Action!" just like they do in the movies about the movies, and we started rolling. We were in it, babes. I hit my lines, Chelsea hit hers, and for a moment we were all breathlessly living in the fantasy of filmmaking. When we finished the scenes, Chelsea called "Cut!" and I smiled. This was going to be fun. Then, Chelsea told DP-fiancé that she wanted to watch playback. Chels, noo, we don't have time. But I didn't say a word because my job was to look pretty and read the lines. Luckily, Tim told her that we didn't have time and the shot looked good. "Let's move on to the next scene," he urged his wife-to-be. But Chelsea wasn't having it. I get it. You can't have your DP *or* your fiancé running the show. Tim, you can't question the director's power in front of her crew. The temperature was warming up, and I could feel the bubblings of tension that so often bleeds into any set.

The next few hours went the same way, with Tim questioning Chelsea's choices and Chelsea snapping back at Tim. The two were bickering the whole day, and it became extremely uncomfortable for everyone. This was only my second movie. I didn't know much about what was right or wrong, appropriate or inappropriate, so I just told myself to go with the flow. My secondary objective, aside from putting on a good performance, was not to cause drama on set. I was sure that once the other, more established actors arrived, things would be ironed out, and luckily, they were on their way.

Milana was the next person to arrive. I love me some Milana Vayntrub. With her there, I knew things would get better, and they did . . . but they were still awkward. In the scene we were shooting with Milana, there was a real live baby involved. I could not believe production got a fresh baby, but Hollywood attracts negligent parents. I swear, y'all. People are willing to give you their fresh babies right out the pussy—placenta perm and all—in return for $85 a day and a shot at fame. Like, really? You're just exposing your baby to the whoop for a chance to be on *Single Parents*?! You wilin', but give me the baby, I have to work.

There's an old Hollywood saying: "Don't act with kids or animals." And Chelsea, a woman who had never directed or written a movie before, felt confident breaking this rule right off the bat. With Milana on set, though, the messiness was beginning to crystallize for me. Milana knew all the right questions to ask, like, "Has this scene been blocked yet?" (*Blocking* is just a fancy industry term for setting up the set, deciding where people will stand, walk, move, so the camera always catches the magic.) On really fancy productions, they hire stand-in actors solely to block the scene so you're not paying those famous fees just to have your stars standing in front of the window while the cameras focus their glare. That's the thing people don't get: Directing is a lot more than action and cut. You're the leader, the main boss. Everything is your responsibility. You need to be prepared: A shot list. Lighting. Cameras. Ego management. Are the actors okay? Do they feel safe? Can they give the best performance? Are the assistants okay? Do they feel safe? Can they give the best performance? Every level of the production from food to emotion to visuals falls on you. Sure, there are teams of professionals brought on to lead each group, but it's your job to lead the whole thing.

When Milana asked whether the scene was blocked yet, Chelsea froze up. She didn't say anything, which meant the answer was obviously no. The scene hadn't been blocked because Chelsea had never had to block a scene before. She'd never directed something of this scale, and it was beginning to show. So Milana, an *experienced* triple threat herself (writer/actor/director), slowly, gently began directing the scene. She was like, "I think Laci should be standing there, and the camera should be over here. Do we see the camera's reflection in the window? We don't need that. Let's drop the blinds. You know what? The baby is crying a lot and the baby isn't even in this shot, so let's have the baby rest for this shot and get clean audio for the editors." It was incredible to watch, and I learned so much.

But at the same time I was like, why is the actor directing and the director standing in the corner biting her nails? I'll give Chelsea this much: you could tell she was relieved to have Milana there guiding the scene. No ego on that girl. (But really, it's also a testament to Milana's talent for directing that she can do it in a way that doesn't make typically fragile directors feel attacked.)

The next day was a travel day, so we hopped on a ferry to head to a remote island. I, as a Black person, should not have gotten on a boat with a bunch of white people headed to a remote island. It was not wise. It felt like I was in a horror film. Oh, wait! I WAS! Oh well, if you get to live, you get to learn. The ferry was dope. As we drove into the ocean, the city floated away in the background, and there was nothing to see but green islands, water, and the horizon. It was peaceful. Beautiful. Some *real* nature shit. When we got to the island, there was a school bus waiting to take us to an *even remoter* part of the island. The school bus was a curious choice, but also shit was rustic as fuck. It fit the vibe.

On the bus, I was *hyped*. At this point, Ally was there—the Squad was multiplying—and I felt like we were doing the damn thing. The actors were so excited to be together, working on a fun movie, that we were dancing in the aisles, doing everything you *wanted* to do on a school bus as a kid but weren't allowed to. The only other person on that bus was the driver, who I also found out was a PA . . . and Chelsea's best friend, Johnny. Chelsea was roping *everybody* into this joint. Ah, the beauty of moviemaking. We're all in this together. Clasps hands. The whole commute gave off a bespoke, summer camp feel. Little did I know that in actuality, this was the opening scene to the horror movie inside the horror movie.

When we got to the resort where the rest of the shoot would be, our excitement reached a fever pitch. As we stepped out of the school bus, the air smelled like dirt and trees and crisp possibilities. It was nothing like smoggy LA. My lungs felt like they had grown three sizes. We had the entire resort to ourselves and each actor was assigned their very own cabin. The whole place had cute little wooden signs that directed you to various nooks and crannies on the property: soaking tubs, sauna, garden, beach, café. It was just about the cutest, hippiest place I'd ever been. As soon as we got on the property, I basically sprinted to my cabin; I couldn't *wait* to see where I'd be staying. When you're coming up in the acting game, you're a piece of meat and nothing else. You're treated horribly because everyone can smell the *want* on your person. You sweat desire and everybody takes advantage of that. Walking into my own cabin tucked into the forest with views of the ocean, I was in disbelief. It takes time to get the star treatment, and I couldn't believe that it was happening to me. It was a real "moving up in the world" moment. I felt glamorous as fuck.

The first day at the resort, we weren't filming, and so Chelsea's dad was like, "Hey, this is one of the most beautiful places in the world. There's this hike where you get the best views on the island; you want me to show it to you?" At this point in the game, it was clear that not only was

Chelsea's dad financing the movie, but he also *owned* the resort we were staying at. The hike sounded fun, but also this dude was king of the castle so it was important to be good sports while we were living our dreams inside *his* castle. We had to play the game. Actors go along and get along, so all three of us agreed without a second thought.

And Phil was right, the hike *was* beautiful. Completely worth the trek to the top. As we were sitting on a rock, taking in the desktop-screensaver views, Phil started talking about his wife, Chelsea's mom, and how they've been married for thirty years. Then he started asking us about our relationships. I wasn't really looking to talk love with a Phish dad I don't really know, so I gave some noncommittal answer (to match my dating style. Lol). Milana also took the vague, noncommittal route and told Phil that she had been in a relationship for a while. Well, Phil latched on. He started asking Milana why she and her partner weren't married, that they really should get married, and then he told her, "Your boyfriend doesn't really love you if he hasn't proposed yet." It was a definite record scratch. Like, um, excuse me, Phil? What are you saying? Milana is a pro and didn't seem bothered by his completely awkward and inappropriate comment. She said something like, "Well, we don't need paperwork to prove we're in love. Not for us." Class act. But the magic of the mountaintop was ruined for sure. We got up, dusted our booties off, and told Phil that we should probably head back to the resort to run our lines. Then Phil went out of pocket.

As we're walking down this hill at a sort of aimless pace, we notice that Phil kept dropping back—first behind Milana, then behind me, then behind Ally. Eventually, we got to a fork in the trail and all spin around to Phil, who is smiling like a maniac. I looked at Milana and Ally, who seemed as confused as I was. Uh, "Philly Cheese Steak, where are we going on this trail?" And this man, I kid you not, says to us, "You guys have to choose." EXCUSE ME, PHIL, WHAT? GET ME OFF THIS FUCKING MOUNTAIN. Things went straight from awkward to straight-up deranged.

Phil took out his iPhone and started filming us. "These actresses are lost in the woods and don't know how to get back. What will happen?!" Okay, I know I said we go along to get along, but we were pretty over Phil at this point.

The three of us wordlessly picked a direction and began walking as Phil trailed behind us. He tried to make conversation the whole time, but we refused to engage. I've never been the same level of furious as three coworkers, but you could tell we were all radiating at the same temp. Milana, Ally, and I marched through the woods, to the soundtrack of twigs snapping under our boots and Phil trying to lighten the mood that he had ruined, while still not actually telling us where to go. We walked and walked. We hit dead ends and circled back. Occasionally, we caught glimpses of the water and knew that if we kept it on the right side of us, we'd be headed in the right direction. We walked for what felt like hours, until we saw signs of life at the end of the snaking trail below. "Congratulations, Ladies," Phil said from behind us. I don't think we even gave him a courtesy chuckle.

We briefly considered going to the soaking tubs to unwind from our stressful event, but all agreed we weren't really in the spa kind of mood so we went our separate ways to try to shake off the day. Back at my star-treatment cabin, all the hiking and fear of being murdered by some white guy had made me really hungry so I decided to walk down to the main restaurant on the resort for a hot meal. I walked into the restaurant on the water, the wood paneling and exposed beams keeping up the rustic summer-camp feel. In the middle was a bar, the familiar rows of wineglasses hanging above the bartender. And under those wineglasses was Phil, with a stiff drink and a ton of paperwork. There was no host, so I went to the bar to ask for a seat, but not before pulling up a chair to make some small talk, you know, be polite in Phil's castle. I sighed and prepared myself. "Doing business?" I asked as I climbed into the barstool next to him. Phil put down the paperwork and picked up his drink. "Yeah, I'm figuring the contracts." "Oh?" I said, "For what?" Phil laughed. "For this movie."

If I had any more record scratches to give, there'd be one right here. But that bitch is all scratched up. I could not believe that this man was figuring out the contracts for the movie we were in the middle of shooting. I could not believe it. But, again, this was only my second movie. And I had learned from shooting *Florida Girls* that contracts actually take a long time to finalize, so long in fact that preproduction is usually in full swing while the suits figure out the numbers. But this wasn't preproduction or a TV show; it was Production with a capital *P* on a movie. We were already well into week one of three, and the contracts weren't figured out? Also, hol up: Phil, our tour guide, resort owner, location manager, Director Daddy, is also the lawyer responsible for drafting up the contract? How? HOW?! I did not have enough energy in my body or food in my belly to deal with this nonsense, so I just wished Phil good luck and went to take my seat by the window. I will say this: the food was bussin. I had the salmon, and it tasted like it was caught right out from the front yard—probably was! I wasn't going to let some sketch lawyering and an eccentric dad get in the way of a good meal.

When Lisa Larsen showed up the next day, we really dove into filming. All the weird juju of the days leading up to her arrival disappeared. Lisa is one of the funniest people I've ever worked with. She is an improv comedy folk hero, a fellow UCB cult member, and an all-around star. Having her on set reminded me why I wanted to do this movie in the first place: to be around talented comedians I could learn from.

In my scene for the day, I had to run around in the woods to escape the killer. I was picked up in a tractor trailer and driven to an even *remoter* part of the island. This is where I really started meeting more of the crew, the other PAs, the hair and makeup team, more of the wardrobe department, and realized this wasn't just *some* friends and family helping out. This was *all* friends and family helping out. Okay, I get it. Blood is thicker than water. In a ruthless industry it's best to surround yourself with people you trust. But also, some people are meant to play one role in your life. We can't let blood relations blind us.

The scene was fairly easy; all I needed to do was run, barefoot, through the woods, scream my head off, and trip. My "costume" was nothing more than a large white shirt, but I was cool with it because all the running and tripping kept my body temp up. There I was, in the woods, running, screaming, tripping—living the dream. We get a few takes in when Tim is like, "Great, we've got it." But of course Chelsea is like, "No, we don't got it. I want to shoot from a different angle." Tim and Chelsea bicker . . . again. (Reminding me a lot again of the doomed couple in the script we were shooting.) They finally settled on strapping a GoPro to my body, *Blair Witch* style, and taking the one real camera they had to a different part of the island to start filming other scenes. So I was left with a few assistants to finish the scene with the GoPro while the rest of the crew headed out.

Even though my legs and feet were getting cut up from running through the woods and my voice was growing hoarse from all the screaming, I was still fueled with the addictive adrenaline of acting in a movie. I was having too much fun to notice any of the amateur-hour shit happening around me. Eventually, we all decided we'd had enough of my running, screaming, and falling and called a wrap on my scenes. That was when I started to notice things. I quickly realized that along with the one camera, the main crew had also left with the tractor trailers, my clothes, and my shoes. I sighed. Mistakes happen, but this felt like a very big mistake. While we were standing around, trying to see if there was any way we could get someone to drive out and give us a ride back to the cabins, a PA took advantage of the rest of the group's distraction to remove the GoPro from my body. "Let me help you with that," he told me as he dove at my back to unhook the rig. His urgency seemed odd, so I made a little joke: "I promise I'm not going to try to steal it." He didn't laugh. "It's not that," he said, and then whispered something in my ear. Turns out, my ass was out the whole time. Cooooooooooolllllllll. Apparently, wearing nothing but a shirt and GoPro results in a booty out situation.

I went from a Japanese-toileted private cabin to going barefoot-ass-out in the woods trying to track down a team of people who drove away with my shoes. This is when I went from feeling "this is weird" to "this isn't right." I knew we were low-budget, but I had been put into a bad situation. It felt like the unprofessionalism had gone too far; a line was crossed. But what was I to do? We were on an island. Do I swim back to the mainland? I didn't want to make waves, literally or metaphorically. At this point, I was still a young and inexperienced actor. When you don't play the game, a bad reputation sticks to you like a tattoo. Ask the lady who played Dr. Izzie Stevens on *Grey's Anatomy*; she'll tell you.

Back at one of the cabins that night, Milana, Lisa, Ally, and I got together with a bottle of wine to start exchanging stories from our day. It sounded like everyone's shoot was just as horrible as mine. Then Milana told us that she had been interested in the script because one of her wildly talented friends from UCB cowrote it, but then, for some reason, his name was taken off the title page and he wasn't involved in production. We all thought this was shady as fuck, but also you will not BELIEVE the amount of shade that goes into almost every Hollywood deal. It's ruthless. People are constantly cutting each other out of everything, even stuff that's already been filmed.

Through some good old-fashioned sleuthing and asking around, we found out that Milana's friend was cut out when it came time to sell the script because neither he nor the studios interested wanted Chelsea to act in and direct the movie—so Chelsea ditched him and decided to do the damn thing herself. Woo, chile, that is just messier than Lionel. Lisa dove at her computer like, "Who is this girl?!" And for the first time since getting involved with the project, we decided to cyberstalk Chelsea. We pulled up her Facebook to see that she had indeed won some sort of scholarship and that's how she got the famous brother duo attached. But as we watched the scholarship video, Lisa's sharp eye noticed that it was stitched together with shoddy editing. Lisa opened her email and sent off a message.

"Who are you emailing?" I asked, giddy with nerves and adrenaline. This had gone from a horror-comedy movie shoot to straight-up spy thriller.

Turns out, Lisa was friends with one of the brothers from the famous brother duo, so she asked him if he knew Chelsea. If you're wondering why we didn't do this in the first place, it's because Hollywood runs on relationships. It's understood that when your reps bring you a project, there's been a level of vetting that's gone into it; our agents are the ones who do the dirty work, the research, the fact-checking, the feeling out whether or not a project is legit. Every movie and TV show has some sort of drama, but you're expected to be loyal to the project in return for the opportunity to create something magical together. But at this point, the gloves were off and loyalty was gone: we'd all been put in too many weird, awkward, and borderline unsafe situations to keep it in the family.

While we were there, drinking and gossiping, Lisa got a response from the brother: "Nope, don't know her. Hope you're well!" Well, hot damn. We all went from thinking we were in a bad situation to *knowing* we were in a bad situation. So what does a group of pretty actors do when they find out they're on an island, involved in a crooked production, led by a director who has no fucking idea what she's doing, bankrolled by a dad who's getting a little too chummy for comfort? They break into the spa. We grabbed our swimsuits and headed through the sleepy resort with nothing but the moonlight guiding our way.

The spa had these three large, incredible outdoor soaking tubs that faced the ocean. As we dipped our toes in, someone—I can't remember who—pointed at the nudity-encouraged sign. Fuck yes. We were all in. Without a word, the four of us stripped away our clothing and jumped into the soaking tubs. It was the hippiest part of the hippiest state, after all, and those soaking tubs were basically built for young, hot, naked bodies escaping from the grind and embracing nature. We were a little wine-drunk and a lot determined to make the best of a shitty situation. And making the best of the situation, at that point, meant a tits-out soak in the moonlight. Sure, we're trapped on this island, brought in under false pretenses, but we're actors— let's have fun with it. Woo! Our only hope was that this movie went direct to Blu-ray and never saw the light of day.

The next day was Tig Notaro Day. Tig was flying in to shoot her scenes, and everyone was on their best behavior. Even though things had been a mess up until that point, I was hopeful that having Tig around would get everything back on track . . . as if there were even a track to get back onto. We were shooting at the main house on the property, the place where Chelsea's parents lived, and when we got there, the house was as incredible as you'd expect—built into the trees with a wraparound deck, showcasing views of the property, the ocean, and the forest. I will say this much, if you're going to be filming a shitty movie where no one knows what they're doing, at least film it somewhere pretty so you have something nice to look at.

When Tig arrived on set, you could tell everyone was really excited to work with her. Tig is an OG. She's the funniest, bluntest person I've ever worked with and one of my favorites on the comedy scene. Tig's character was hilarious, and her scene was simple but a knockout. Without giving away too many identifying details, Tig's character provided a lot of the comedy to the horror part of the movie. Eventually, at the end of her scene, my character was supposed to basically kick her out of the house. So we began filming, but this time, my excitement quickly gave way to the incompetence: Mic packs were sticking out of pants and visible on camera. The bickering between Chelsea and her DP-fiancé was at an all-time high. We didn't know where to stand or walk to make sure we didn't ruin the shot. It was sloppy.

When it came time for my character to kick Tig's character out, we set up the shot so the camera was on Tig to get her reaction. So Tig does her lines, a total pro—she was crushing it—and then I stood up, behind the camera, and said mine. At which point, Chelsea yelled, "Cut!" and Tim yelled, "We got it! That's a wrap on Tig." As quickly as the scene started, it ended, and I knew we definitely didn't "got it," because the camera wasn't on me, which means they don't have footage of my character saying the line, which you always need for the edit. At this point, I was getting used to these things, but I was at least hoping they'd get their shit together enough for my scene with Tig. I'd assumed there'd be *some* video proof that she and I were ever in the same room, filming at the same time together. But NOPE.

The one saving grace was Tig's IRL departure. Since she'd only had to film that one scene, she'd flown in on a seaplane and was flying out immediately afterward. As she was getting ready to head to her plane, she took one look at us, the motley crew, and said, "See you at the Oscars!" before walking off into the horizon. It was the funniest, most badass thing I've ever seen in my life. And if I'd had any wits about me, I would've Mission Impossibled that shit, packed my bags, hooked my scarf around the wheels, and Tom Cruised my way right out of there with her.

During our lunch break that day, we were sitting around and chatting when the crew began to pack up and leave. Something felt off. The crew was quiet, angry. No one was having fun anymore. If your crew is unhappy, then you're *really* in trouble. Also, crew people are on the tea and I needed the tea. So I asked a PA what was up. This was when I learned that he had flown in on his own dime and had yet to be reimbursed. He also shared that there was no per diem, and no one on the crew had gotten paid yet. Uh-oh. This was bad. Very bad. I had to figure out how to tell the other actors without alerting Chelsea or her parents.

Toward the end of lunch, Chelsea told us they wanted to get some establishing shots without us "real quick." I rolled my eyes, because nothing about this production was "real quick." But again, we were not in a position to tell her how to run things, so we just stayed put in this enormous house that wasn't ours. Chelsea headed off with Tim and some of the crew, while we just hung out. I caught up the girlies with what was happening, and everyone kind of decided that we should probably make a game plan to get out of this situation, but first, we had to at least get out of (one of) her parents' house(s). An hour went by and Chelsea was nowhere to be found, so we pulled out some board games. Then an hour went by and we got bored with the board games, so we began milling about. At this point, Ally went out onto the balcony to take in the views, and we heard,

"OH MY GOD. GUYS, LOOK AT THIS." We walk out to see what they were talking about, and sure enough, through the clearing down below was a perfect sight line to the outdoor soaking tubs—the same ones we had been naked in the night before. Anyone who lived at the house, and stood out at that balcony, could very clearly take in whoever was in the naked soaking tubs. It almost felt like the two structures were built specifically for voyeurism. And my immediate thought was: Oh my god, did Phil see us in our titty-out moonlight séance situation? IS PHIL A PERV?! In that moment, on that balcony, we went from idly thinking about an escape plan to making an escape plan.

Not wanting anyone to overhear us speaking negatively about the set we were currently living in, we decided to ask Chelsea's head PA/best friend to drive us into town for a little actor bonding dinner. He agreed, so we loaded up on the school bus one more time, the ride a little less gleeful than before, and headed to a secret meeting of the minds. The great thing about Chelsea's PA bestie is he was chatty as fuck, so it was very easy to get more details out of him. I was straight up like, "Hey, I heard the girls aren't getting paid . . . What's up with that?"

He didn't even try to lie. "Yeah, we're having issues with wardrobe and makeup. We didn't realize doing gore cost so much more money. So we're trying to figure out how much more we have." No shit, dude. It's high art to make a bitch look busted. People get degrees for that kind of talent. The dude went on. "It's all just such a mess. Chelsea is my best friend, but I'm not sure she's even going to marry Tim." He told us *everything*: how she'd never really directed before, how she had run out of money. *You're supposed to be her best friend. How are you telling us all her business?* The bus ride into town was exactly long enough for us to confirm that there was no way we could go forward with this project.

As soon as Messy McBestie was back on the bus and headed back to the resort, we began to really plan our escape. Thank God for Lisa, who had some power and was comfortable speaking up. "If you guys are cool with it," she told us over pizza, "I don't mind being the bad guy and calling my reps." Calling reps meant quitting, but no one would ever use that word because it's a bad look. That's why we have reps who *represent* our interests, and our interests were to GTFO. Milana, who also had power, agreed and said she'd call her reps too. At the time, Milana and I had the same reps, so I knew if they were pulling her out, they'd pull me out too. With the pizza eaten and our reps called, we felt a little ripple of relief—enough to even get ice cream. If you looked at us from afar, we really appeared to be a crew of young creatives having an idyllic evening out while working hard at their craft. We were actually living it up as hostages.

While I may have gotten into acting to entertain the masses and snatch some of that star-quality privilege for myself, I've stayed in acting because of people like Lisa, Milana, Ally, and Tig. These are professionals who always look out for the crew, for the team, and who are also funny as fuck. Although the movie was shaping up to be a nightmare, the new friends *almost* made running through the forest ass out over and over again worth it.

When PA McBestie dropped us back off at the cabins that night, we all huddled in Lisa's room while we waited for our reps to go nuclear on Chelsea and her production (aka her parents). We knew that with no cast, there was no movie, and it was gut-wrenching to wait for the bomb to drop. As we did, we heard some commotion outside of Lisa's cabin. All four of us ran to the windows and peeked through blinds only to see a real live mutiny unfolding. The costume designer was standing in the middle of the cabins cussing out Chelsea as loud as possible. Soon the sound team was coming out, yelling about how they were packing their bags and leaving. After a while it felt like everyone involved was outside, yelling at Chelsea. Sloppy. It was giving *Succession*, but with hippies.

While we're watching all this unfold, Chelsea eventually turns from the growing mob and runs into Lisa's cabin crying. It was clear that at some point between dinner and Chelsea coming into the cabin, the news of our leaving was broken to her. "Please," she sobbed, "what can I do to get you to stay?" I could've killed my reps then (who are not my reps now) for not handling it more delicately. We literally pay them to be the bad guy so we never have to. We pay them to do our dirty work. And here was Chelsea, sobbing in front of all of us, while we squirmed in our skin. Since Lisa and Milana had been the ones to get the ball rolling on our escape, I decided that I'd take one for the team and guide Chelsea away from the others.

I walked her down to the water, where it was private and beautiful and told her straight up, "Listen, Chels, this isn't how stuff works. If someone's representatives call to say it's over, then it's over. It's not appropriate to confront them." Chelsea began to cry even harder, spiraling over every life decision that had brought her to that point. I really felt for her in the moment, because it was clear this girl was in over her head and her parents should've never handed her a movie budget.

I pulled her in for the best bosom hug I could muster with these 36C titties. You know, they're not Oprah titties, but you can still cry on them. But it was over. Chelsea knew it. I knew it. The whole crew knew it. The next day we packed up and boarded a seaplane without looking back. I was so terrified the seaplane was going to crash and the headlines would read "Lisa Larsen, Milana Vayntrub, and Others Die in Watery Plane Crash." I was too far down the call sheet to die! I didn't want to be remembered as "and Others." But luckily, the flight went smoothly.

We'd escaped. It sucked. The whole thing: the movie, the awkward situations, being taken hostage on an island, watching Chelsea's dream (and maybe relationship?) crumble before our very eyes.

That's the problem with the whole "blood is thicker than water" thing: sometimes that blood isn't the right type for what you need. Putting loyalty to your family above all else opens up vulnerabilities. I genuinely don't think Chelsea and her family were trying to run a fraudulent film, but all of the corner-cutting and white lies added up to a fractured reality. Even though filmmaking is all about bringing a fantasy world to life, you have to ground the production in reality if you're ever going to make a good one and treat the cast and crew with the respect they deserve in the process. This family was not grounded in *any* sort of reality.

Of all the scams to run, I resonate with family scams the most. We're all getting smarter about the power of boundaries, but again, how do you set boundaries with people who birthed you? With the people who will go to any lengths to keep you happy, fed, alive? If anything, a family that scams together and/or for each other, to me, is a sign of a very strong family. We should be so lucky to have parents who hand over their wallets, their homes, their resorts, and their legal acumen to help actualize our dreams. Scamilies will never be able to see outside their own love for each other to understand how their shitty, protective behavior impacts those around them. That's why it's up to you to never trust a rich family funding each other's fantasies . . . only the mom-and-pop shops. I'm telling you.

Romance Scams

ike all humans, scammers are multidimensional people with different motives. Some scam for noble reasons, like Robin Hood; that little fox was taking from the blue-blooded to give to the poor. Others scam for social reasons, like me fooling people (including myself) into thinking I know what I'm doing. Then there's a subset of scammers who do it for the sick and twisted pathological pleasure of emotionally harming another person's heart. I call these the romance scammers. Romance scammers are vile. Yes, I fuck with scams, but the scams I like are the ones where the little man scams the big man or the weird ones where no one gets hurt. Romance scams are a different breed, and they . . . are . . . everywhere.

In fact, I've found in my extremely unscientific Scam U studies that 97 percent of dudes between the ages of twenty and thirty-two are romance scammers. That's the truth. I've dated men and women in a lot of different places—Texas,

Pittsburgh, New York, Los Angeles—and so I have a lot of experience in this field. Let me tell you, it's trash everywhere. Particularly in LA, where dating is like parking: you're just never going to find an empty spot. You have to circle the block a few times, follow a person to their car, or wait until you see someone backing out and be like, "Are you leaving? Can I get in there?" Sometimes, like my friend Joel Kim Booster says, "You have to settle for a Bird scooter."

It's the most natural thing on earth to want love. Who wants to live a life of no passion? Certainly not this bitch. All of us want love, which leaves us vulnerable to cons. Care is the currency in romantic scams. Like I've said before, if you try to *will* a situation into being, if you want something too badly, you can become ignorant to what you actually need. And this need-ignorance can make you love-dumb, like poor Benita Alexander in this next story.

DR. DUPE

If you squint real good and take a few swings of the strong stuff, Swiss-born Italian surgeon Paolo Macchiarini kind of looks like George Clooney . . .'s less-attractive older brother. What he's lacking in actor good looks, he's made up for in his surgery skills. He was cutting up all types of important people in his heyday: Bill and Hillary Clinton, Emperor Akihito of Japan, and President Obama. Y'all, he was cutting on Barry! Okay, Paolo. I see you.

In 2008, Paolo became known to the world after he used experimental regenerative medicine—you know, the stem-cell stuff—to create and install a new trachea for a young mother named Claudia from Barcelona. The thing is, this type of transplant had never been done before until Paolo was crazy enough to try it. After Claudia not only survived but went on to live a normal life—which included showing off her new throat while clubbing in Ibiza; you go, Claudia!—Paolo's medical breakthrough was covered around the globe. Paolo would eventually go on to regenerate seventeen windpipes in total. He was givin' all the girls new throats!

In around 2013, Paolo's pioneering work landed him in front of Meredith Vieira's production team at NBC News who thought his inspiring story was absolutely perfect for a documentary. Damn, remember when documentaries were inspiring and thought-provoking? Now they're all about nice white ladies being defrauded out of money or nice white ladies disappearing or nice white ladies being murdered—which is basically the same as disappearing. Anyway . . . during the production of the documentary *A Leap of Faith*, Paolo struck up a friendship with NBC News producer Benita Alexander.

Benita, an Emmy Award–winning investigative journalist, was going through a tough time. Paolo was going through his own difficult time too: he and his wife were in the process of divorcing. Benita later told *20/20*, "He was an amazing friend to me during that time, and a solid, reliable pillar of strength. He spent hours listening to me talk about it all and offering gentle advice."

Well, we all see where this is going, cuz nothing's more romantic than trauma bonding! Paolo and Benita's friendship eventually turned into a relationship. (I'm no journalist, butttt doesn't that break all sorts of rules, Benita? Aren't y'all not even allowed to accept water from someone you're interviewing? How are you going to touch nasties? I guess if you're giving everyone throat, you deserve some throat too!) During postproduction of *A Leap of Faith* Paolo and Benita's whirlwind romance became a worldwide romance with trips to the Bahamas, Turkey, Mexico, Greece, and Italy where they went on shopping sprees and ate their way through Michelin-starred restaurants.

Then one day, floating through the ocean on a dinner cruise, Paolo shared some exciting news with Benita: his divorce had been finalized, and he was an unattached man. Dude popped the question right there, ballin' on a boat in the seas. According to Benita, Paolo said, "I want to surprise you with a wedding in Italy. Just find your dress. I will plan everything else." A true king.

Soon, the (surprise) wedding planning began. And this is Wedding with a capital *W* because shit was extravagant. They set a date for July 11, 2015, in Rome, and throughout the planning process, Benita got little hints of what was to come: The guest list included the Obamas (♥), the Clintons, and America's other lovable leader Vladimir Putin. The wedding was going to be catered by Enoteca Pinchiorri, a three-Michelin-star restaurant. Elton John would play the rehearsal dinner; Andrea Bocelli would sing at the ceremony (both

Kim *and* Kourtney would be PISSED); and John Legend was booked to play the reception. Yo, Paolo, you are bad at keeping a secret! All I hear is all these damn names clanking around the floor. The most impressive name clanking? The wedding would be officiated by one of Paolo's patients: THE MOTHERFUCKING POPE. Not only did Pope Francis offer to officiate, but he also offered up his summer castle as a venue. Hey, Paolo, can you, um, plan my wedding? Let me just find someone right quick.

And then it all fell apart. Fast. Like these things always do. One of Benita's friends sent her an article about how Pope Francis would be doing his papal stuff in South America on July 11. And if that date looks familiar to you, it's because it's the same damn day Benita and Paolo were supposed to be getting married by the pope in his palace. I mean, he must've been dicking her down good if she thought *the pope* was going to Airbnb out his crib and officiate for her. Benita put her journalist hat back on and hired a private investigator, who started following Paolo around and eventually discovered that everything he said was a lie. *Oh dang, so no Barack doing the Cha Cha Slide?*

The PI's simple review of public records uncovered that Paolo was still married to his wife of thirty years, and they had a daughter and son. And, y'all, this is where the bad gets worse. Remember all that groundbreaking surgery Paolo was doing? Well, it turns out that his throats weren't as popping as we all thought. Aside from the few like Claudia who went on to live normal lives, many of his patients faced severe complications from their surgery, some that were fatal. So not only did he scam Benita and play down his controversial methods for NBC, but he conned the entire medical industry. Ooof.

You guys know I fuck with con artists hard, but I do not fuck with this. Nope. A fundamental part of being a human is love—needing physical touch and connection to survive. That's why nice, smart investigative journalists get scammed into thinking Elton John's going to belt out some "Tiny Dancer" at their rehearsal dinners. Preying on the need for love is the most disgusting thing you can do as a person—and unfortunately, for many of us, we've been in the position where we've been preyed upon. I know I have. Con-gregation, let me tell you a story.

VALENTINE'S DAZE

I've been dating for over ten years—and not that hard. My ideal person would be someone who God just brings to my couch, who can give me that good, think-free fucking. But so far, that hasn't happened. So occasionally, I have a lapse in judgment and go on a date. To be honest, though, even when I click with someone on a date, I find it hard to open up.

My whole career is about managing rejection. Dealing with and adapting to disappointing news is my full-time job. I'm constantly trying to fight the odds and achieve very difficult goals. I'm used to every moment of every day being a challenge, so when something feels difficult, it becomes more interesting to me. Because of this, I've had to develop some thick-ass skin to survive, but unfortunately, that makes it hard to open myself up to other people in my personal life. Besides, I don't want to shed this tough skin! It photographs so well, and I worked hard to grow it. But not letting anyone in to see the real me makes dating difficult. I know firsthand, though, that if you cut yourself off from too much love and care, you might forget what it looks like.

Just this past year, I had a date with a C-list celebrity. This is a litigious motherfucker so *all* identifying details have been changed. You can stop trying to figure out who it is and just join me on this journey.

This guy—I'll call him Michael—and I had seen each other around at work functions here and there. One day, he reached out and asked if I wanted to get dinner with him while he was in town. I enthusiastically said yes. I am unapologetically one of those "dating as a celebrity is hard" kind of people. In general, dating is all about lining up your wants and needs to complement your partner's wants and needs. It's difficult to strike the right balance, and when you live a big, shiny life of unquenchable ambition—finding balance can be outright impossible. I hadn't dated many people who would understand my schedule and needs, but I figured that someone like Michael would totally get it. So we set a time and place to meet up for dinner, which happened to be his last night in LA. *Cool,* I thought, *I'm the headliner of his weekend.*

When it came time to meet, I ordered an Uber to be all prompt . . . and it canceled last second. By the time another one took my ride, it was peak traffic. I was behind the eight ball. It wasn't Pride, but I still blame the gays! I was thirty minutes late and sure I would be fired. The second I saw him, I could tell that he was not having it. It was probably the first time I'd ever seen this dude scowl. Michael was mean mug-

SCAM LIFE LESSON
Everyone likes talking about themselves, even people who say they don't.

ging me to the core, and to be honest, I deserved it. I knew he was a busy man with limited time to waste, and here I was, rolling up late on a little bit of mushrooms. Wrong foot, my bad.

I knew it was time to turn on my Laci charm. So I turned to what every A-B-C-D-list celebrity loves to talk about: themselves. If you ever want to reset the energy or turn down the temperature of an interaction, just ask the person you're talking to a personal question, because **everyone likes talking about themselves, even people who say they don't**. It's the fastest way to get people to like you.

"Has it been hard balancing all your various projects, or do you like working at this pace?" I asked Michael while browsing the menu. Dude went off. He started with what inspired him to get into entertainment in the first place, then he moved on to what he sees for himself in the future, then on to how he was going through a difficult time at work/he wasn't getting the recognition he deserved/he didn't feel his reps were doing enough for him, and on and on.

He talked for twenty minutes, then thirty, then forty. He kept it up through the dessert course until I realized that he had not asked me one single question about myself. I hadn't spoken more than a few "mhms" and "wows" in almost an hour.

I spent the whole meal drifting off in my head while making sure to throw in an occasional, "Oh, really? That's wild," so he didn't know how hard I had checked out. It was probably the lack of engagement (or the mushrooms), but I really spaced out, thinking about love and dating and how difficult it was to connect with people. For me. For everyone. It felt like globally, people were having trouble connecting even though tools to get in touch were stronger than ever. You could talk to a person across the country in an instant, but for some reason it felt like everyone everywhere was struggling with quality connections. At the time, I was watching a lot of *Love on the Spectrum* on Netflix. It's this wonderful show that follows different people on the autism spectrum as they navigate love and companionship. Big recommend. *Love on the Spectrum* breaks down the difficulty of dating in a refreshing way. Through the lens of autism, we see that there are endless subtle microgestures that go into communicating with a person. Just because someone smiles at you doesn't mean they want to kiss you, and just because someone wants to kiss you doesn't mean they'll smile at you. Seeing all the maddening social intricacies unpacked on a glossy Netflix show made me realize how impossible it is to get a read on a person. What I really dig about *Love on the Spectrum* is that, ultimately, it's a show about demystifying love; it's about how the basis for love is the same for everyone across community, culture, and life experience.

"You know," I said, coming out of my trance, "dating isn't that difficult; it's basically just making a new friend."

Well, reader, any progress I had made with Michael disappeared right then and there. He just completely clammed up. No more work talk. No more self-talk. Nothing. He asked for the check, and the date was over after one of the iciest hugs in my life. I felt horrible. He clearly thought, "Not only did this bitch show up late to the date, but now she's trying to friend-zone me?!"

When I got home, I immediately sent him a text: *Hey, sorry about tonight. I was off my game. Cancel your flight and try again tomorrow?* 😊

I hate it when people are disappointed in me. I hate fucking up a social situation. I hate making someone feel shitty. I've dedicated my life to doing comedy so that everyone always has fun when I'm around, and I didn't do that here. I sent that text because I wanted to salvage my reputation with Michael. Honestly? I wish I never had. I wish I had taken the lack of chemistry as a sign that it wasn't right. But I'm a Cancer. I nurture. I ingratiate. I seek security where there's none to be had.

To my surprise, my cute text worked. Michael actually canceled his flight home to spend the next day with me. Flips hair, pops hip: Laci Charm! I wanted this dude to know I wasn't a complete asshole. I know how to have a good time and treat a person right; it's just that sometimes I take mushrooms earlier in the day and move a little slower than usual.

During our redo, we went on one of those glorious twenty-four-hour dates that starts with brunch and ends with deep late-night diner conversations about your upbringing. We began at Harriet's: a cool rooftop bar on the Sunset Strip in Hollywood. It's across from LA's iconic Comedy Store and overlooks the skyline, which means this spot has allllll the vibes. You could fall in love with a tree while watching the sun soak into the U.S. Bank Tower. At Harriet's, we ran into some mutuals—which always feels good. I don't care who you are, what you do, or where you live, when you're out on the town and you run into people you know and love, it is the best. Maybe I just love it because it's such a rarity when you live in big cities like LA or New York. But running into people you know in front of a date always carries clout. For the people you know to also know your date? Well, everyone's going to be vibing off each other then!

Our friends pulled up seats, ordered drinks, and we proceeded to look and act like we were in one of those life-changing pharma commercials. You know, the part where everyone's having the time of their lives distracting you from the list of side effects the narrator is rattling off.

Soon, we ordered another round of drinks, and things began to get even more loose. Michael gave me a lap dance in a cute and goofy way, and I began to see it: a possibility of a relationship forming. I liked Michael. He was really funny and silly. Extra. Magnetic. He was confident in himself and didn't care if he looked corny in public. Anything for a laugh. More drinks were ordered. I was giving him a lap dance this time. Because I'm really funny and silly. Extra. Magnetic. I'd also do anything for a laugh. On top of it, we had jumped from an awkward first date to day-drinking with friends . . . it felt like we were on a sped-up relationship timeline. All in all, it was seeming like a match made in Hollywood Heaven.

The next day, Michael and I were exchanging flirty texts when he mentioned he'd checked to see if there were any photos or videos from our twenty-four-hour date online. *Oh, haha*, I said, all but brushing off the fact that he was googling himself. Michael didn't take the hint and continued to share how he was really disappointed to see that no one posted anything to the gossip sites. I found myself having an "Um, What?" moment. Like, maybe he wasn't as self-assured as I initially thought. But the reality was, we were both working in the entertainment industry, and I know better than anyone how hard it is to turn off the performance aspect of your identity. We're all performing anyway—especially when in public, on a date. I let the comment slide and we continued to text.

Every time Michael was in town, we'd get together, and eventually, we were in a full-blown relationship. Visits became more frequent and planned. We'd spend all our free time together. I liked being with Michael because he understood my wants and needs; he knew how I was wired and didn't care about my work schedule because he was juggling the same one. Even though the honeymoon phase was going strong, there was one strange thing that was becoming difficult to ignore: after every whirlwind visit, I'd find myself emotionally and spiritually drained. I assumed that's what being in a long-distance relationship felt like: an intense period, followed by a crash. But as one month turned to two, then three and four, I began to wonder how sustainable these intense relationship highs and lows would be. Just when I thought that maybe it *wasn't* normal to feel exhausted every time you spent a weekend with your man, he told me he was moving to Los Angeles.

Y'all, I was so excited! All my energy problems would be solved. Now that he was going to be in Los Angeles, we wouldn't have to pack a full-ass relationship into a short-ass weekend. As Michael was relocating and we were spending more time together, I began to notice that maybe we weren't as similar as I initially thought. For one, he seemed to have a lot more patience for the outside world than I do. He always wanted to go out for every meal together. Don't get me wrong: I love to eat out, but your girl gets tired. Sometimes a chill meal at home is better than what any restaurant can offer you. We could never go out for a casual meal either; he always insisted I had my full face on, *just in case* we were photographed together. I vividly remember being at a restaurant after one of my fifteen-hour workdays and I was so exhausted that I began falling asleep at the table. Even though I'd asked for a chill night in, Michael said that we should go out and firmly urged that I keep my makeup on from work.

At dinner, as my eyes began to shut and my head tilted forward, he snapped at me, "Hey! Look up! Look happy when we're out together." *Look happy when we're out together?* Of course, in retrospect and seeing that in writing, it gives me the ick. What kind of partner demands you pretend to look like you're happy when you're tired? A normal human response to the situation would've been, "Hey, boo, are you okay? You looked exhausted." But instead, he was like, snapping in my face, telling me to "Look chipper!" On the one hand, the performer, the con artist in me, respected the hustle. What did that one white guy in that one white movie about those white hustlers say? Always be closing? Yeah. That. But on the other hand, I'm a human person who was fucking tired. I didn't need my partner dehumanizing me out at dinner. I needed him to STFU and tuck me into bed. I didn't want to be chasing clout; I wanted to eat and sleep like a regular person.

Now look, the storybook version of Laci would recognize that this dude was exhibiting behavior I do not like . . . She'd also recognize that she had already had many experiences in her life that proved she should trust her gut. But this isn't storybook Laci, or even actor Laci: this is real Laci—the one who fucks up all the time. I'm a hyper-self-aware person, but I can tell you right here and now that I do not follow my own advice. I'm a scammer; I'm a performer; I'm a con artist. My career depends on people liking me, and it's hard to turn that off in the dating world. I come to every date like, "Look how interesting I am. Look how good I am on paper. Like me, like me, like me!" The problem is with this particular motherfucker, he was just as charming as I am. All our friends loved us together; they thought Michael and I were a perfect fit. I didn't want to let anyone down with my doubts about him. I wanted to fit the bright and shiny narrative that those closest to me were spinning. I wanted to be the performer, the snake charmer. So I kept dating the snake.

This next part is shitty and sucks to write, but I want to convey that even Scam Goddesses can get played—especially when it comes to romance. So here we go.

One day, we were hanging out at his spot when, out of nowhere, Michael slapped me across the face. Hard. When I say "out of nowhere," I mean literally out of thin air. One moment I was walking up the stairs, passing Michael on my way up, and the next my cheek was burning. It happened so randomly that at first I thought something fell from the ceiling and caught my face on the way down. That was a more plausible scenario than this man that I loved, this man I wasn't even fighting with, would raise a hand to my face . . . just to see if he could.

I lifted my hand to my cheek and felt the burn of his palm across my beautiful, moneymaking face. The same one he made me cover in makeup and plaster with a smile whenever there was a possibility that a camera might be on us. I couldn't believe it. As soon as I realized that it wasn't the fucking sky falling down onto my head, but instead a cruel act from the man I loved, my confusion turned to unhinged rage.

"WHAT THE FUCK?" I screamed. "WHAT THE FUCK DID YOU DO THAT FOR?" His shoulders raised into his ears, in a mea culpa kind of stance, but his words didn't match. "It was just a joke," he said nonchalantly, turning away from me and walking toward his bedroom. No apology. No "Are you okay?" Just . . . *a joke*. Now, I've been doing comedy and improv for the better part of a decade. I know how to write a joke, make a joke, take a joke, and perform a joke. Physical abuse was never a joke bucket anyone reached into, especially anyone with talent. Michael plodded over to his bed, casually, like he hadn't just randomly hit me in the face. My rage burned on, but the confusion was still there too. I could not comprehend what had just happened.

Later, when I told my cousin Eric (anytime you see "cousin," it's Eric) about his odd behavior and the whole "joke" thing, he cut off the conversation then and there with a simple: "Michael is grooming you for abuse." I knew what the phrase meant, but I still couldn't imagine that it related to me. I was strong. I was vocal. I was funny. I was known. How could someone groom *me* for abuse? The whole situation was so unbelievable that I just didn't believe it. I continued seeing Michael. I figured it was a one-off thing: maybe his brain shorted; maybe his arm had a spasm; maybe he struggled with Tourette's and didn't tell me. Maybe. Maybe. Maybe. I made up any story to make sense of what was happening. But what was happening was that he was practicing abuse. He started out with little ways of controlling my looks, my energy, the where and how of me eating, and then moved up to physical violence to see if he could get away with it. I so wish that this was what ended our relationship, but what really ended it was a bouquet of flowers.

Scamming is a double-edged sword.

On Valentine's Day, I hit Michael up to see if he wanted to do something. "Yeah, maybe, I'll see if I'm free" was all he said. This weird, noncommittal answer bummed me the fuck out, but I would've never admitted it. So I just took my ass to the gym on the first floor of my building. This was yet another example of my need to mask myself for the comfort of others. I didn't see it at the time, but honestly, as I write it all out here, it becomes clearer and clearer. The whole scam of scamming is that if you're too good at it, you begin to con yourself out of real human connection. So buyer beware: **scamming is a double-edged sword**.

I was running on the treadmill when I got a notification on my phone that someone was at my door. I watched the short clip from my doorbell camera to see a delivery person leaving a huge bouquet of flowers. I rolled my eyes, thinking, *Michael is so corny doing something shady and then getting me flowers, as if I'm that easy.* I didn't even bother going upstairs. *Let someone steal them*, I thought, and kept on running.

When I was finished with my workout, I took the elevator up to deal with The Flowers. When I got to the door, I saw that the bouquet looked even bigger and more beautiful in person. As I lifted the surprisingly heavy vase, I noticed the note tucked inside. *This had better be good*, I thought. I opened it up:

> Happy Valentine's Day, sending you
> lotsa love. —Mary

Mary. My person I call when I'm dying and need a ride to the ER Mary. My white girlfriend Mary. My friend you want by your side when shit goes down Mary. She knew things were rough with Michael, and she took a moment out of her day and some money out of her wallet (flowers are so expensive, you guys, why?) to send me a floral hug. It was one of the purest displays of love that I have ever received. Nothing transactional. No motive other than letting me know that she loved me. It was love so strong, it cured me of Michael's toxicity. The veil was lifted, and I couldn't unsee how hateful he'd been toward me.

Mary's gesture *instantly* turned my Valentine's Day around. I was like, fuck this shit. Fuck this guy. It's going to be all about me, myself, and I tonight. Earlier that day I'd seen an incredible-looking Valentine's Day meal on my favorite cooking channel: TikTok. So I decided *that* was how I was going to spend my night, making myself a delicious meal because I deserved it. I marched on over to Whole Foods to grab my ingredients, along with a nice bottle of Sauvignon Blanc. (The recipe was a lobster lettuce wrap with mango salsa and I really thought, *Bitch, I'm about to be Chef Boyardee*—but of course, it was Valentine's Day and everybody was sucking down lobster, so Whole Foods was fresh out. I settled for shrimp instead.) I paid a million-thousand dollars because Whole Foods is bougie as fuck and headed home to COOK.

Spending Valentine's Day with myself, cooking a meal for me, with no makeup on, my real hair out, was actually . . . kind of life-changing. Mary's kindness paired with my independence reminded me what real, true love looked like and, more important, felt like. I felt good in my body that night, even though a bad relationship was ending. I felt lighter. Freer. In control. If you can swing it, I highly recommend cooking a nice meal for yourself and ONLY YOU on Valentine's Day. Shortly thereafter, I ended things with Michael, the vain, C-list celebrity, clout chaser, experimental abuser, and got to work identifying and rebuilding my boundaries.

There's always a lot of victim-blaming going on when someone gets duped by a partner. There's almost an arrogance that goes on. We get fed the same type of boring narrative about what a victim looks like. That's why most people think, *Oh, this can't happen to me, this happens on* Dateline. *I'm too smart to be hurt by someone like that. I know better.* Even survivors of abuse who are brave enough to step up and speak out are often characterized as weak or conniving or untruthful or, in the best-case scenario, they're just flattened to a 2D representation of their trauma. This is exactly why violence is so pervasive. We don't humanize the people who have gone through it, and therefore, we don't see ourselves within them.

We are told abuse looks a certain way, that it happens to a certain person and is committed by certain people, but the truth is: it's not as concrete as that; there's no certainty to it. Not a single person enters a relationship thinking, *I might get hit in the face.* There's no way to prepare for the hurt that someone you love can unleash on you. I'm my favorite person, but I still got conned into wasting my time with a scrub who was testing the waters of being an abuser. This has nothing to do with me and everything to do with him. The only way to be 100 percent certain you'll never experience harm from a person you love is to never love in the first place. And that's no way to live.

Being loved is a fundamental need for humans. We need to have the door a little bit open to let a stranger in because that stranger could potentially become a friend, a partner, a love. But all the conventional stories about how to "get love" often start from the wrong perspective. There are endless books, shows, and podcasts about people looking for or finding love, because if someone can't be in a relationship, then something is wrong with them. (Bullshit.) These pieces of pop culture throw everything at the wall. Play coy. Don't text too soon. Wear something tight. Don't text too much. Laugh. Don't talk about exes. All of these rules don't take into account YOUR experience, YOUR needs, YOUR wants. I guess, if you are to take away any lessons from this chapter—and feel free not to follow them like I do—I guess they'd be this: dating isn't about how much the person likes you; it's all about how much you like them. We're trained to flirt, to please, to be lovable. But really, we need to focus on what we need and whether the person in front of us is meeting that need. My only advice when it comes to dating, and I've done a lot of it, is to listen. First, listen to your instincts; listen to what your body tells you. Next, listen to what your date is saying. Let people talk about themselves, and they'll pretty quickly show you their true character. Learn who you are first, and that will help you see who other people really are. And remember: **no one gets to tell you who you are**.

SCAM LIFE LESSON

No one gets to tell you who you are.

The Scammer's Tool Kit

I hope that, at this point, you are well versed in the various types of scams that exist in the world. I said it once, and I'll say it again: everything in life is a scam. The sooner you accept this truth, the sooner you'll be able to start living the life you've always wanted. When I learned this valuable lesson, the world opened up to me in the most unexpected of ways. I began to recognize opportunities and see pathways that were previously invisible to the overachieving, rule-following eye. I might be sounding like some sort of hippie-dippie LA girl here, but life is all about finding creative ways to manifest the things you want. If you take anything away from this book, it should be that there's no right way to get from Point A to Point B. Anyone who claims to hold the easy answer to anything you want out of life—a connection to faith, job security, a dope housing situation, success, friendship, body acceptance, a functional family, love, whatever—is a goddamn scammer. And that's okay! Because I'm a scammer too. We all should be playing the game, trying to get what we want and need out of this life.

Here's why I run scams: because the world is imbalanced. Look around. It's an unfair place. The people who signed, sealed, and delivered the social contract we're all expected to abide by did a horrible job. Dig deep enough and you'll find every major system in place is built on a shitty foundation. It's all crumbling anyway: ask anyone who works in health care, education, legal justice . . . fuck, even the entertainment industry is crumbling. As I type this, we're all on strike. By the time you read it, maybe we'll have to be again. I am being actively barred from my *favorite* scam because a small group of blue-blooded suits are obsessed with control.

That's why I love running scams. I see them as small opportunities to bring a little fairness back into the fold. Turning on my scammer brain has helped me get out of bad situations and into good ones. It's how I got deemed the Scam Goddess—and I wouldn't be a true Scam Goddess if I weren't a benevolent bitch. So I want to leave you with my favorite hoodwinks: a refresher of the scams in these pages, a few I run in my day-to-day to make my life better and brighter. When we do eventually part, I hope you'll have everything you need to bring more balance into the world. Because this bitch really does need balance.

SCAM TIP #1:
OPERATE FROM THE BEST OUTCOME

Real-deal scammers go into every situation assuming that the best thing is going to happen to them—even when they don't know *how* exactly that "best thing" will happen. Operating from the best outcome is a popular scam in show business, too. People are always pitching TV shows they have no clue how to make. If your pitch is convincing, if you talk like the show already exists and you're the only person on earth who can create it, you might get paid a ton of money to make it, regardless of your experience and skill level.

Living life where you operate from the best outcome means the best outcome is going to come your way one way or another. For example, every time I get ready to go out with my girls, I do it up like I'm about to party with red-carpet royalty. Even when I was a nobody who had zero connections and zero business being around celebrities, I still carried myself like I was going to have the best night ever, because shoot, maybe I was! Sure enough, one night, I was out with my girls at the 40/40 Club, and who the fuck walks in? Queen Bey herself. My ultimate girl. I couldn't believe it—okay, okay, fine, Jay-Z owns the club, so it might've been strategic positioning—but still, I was HYPED. Beyoncé. Right in front of me. Walking toward me, walking past me, walking away from me, walking up to VIP, walking out of my life. I looked over at my gorgeous crew, all in black dresses, eyes trained on the empty space that once held the greatness who had just breezed past, and got an idea. "DO AS I DO!" I yelled over the music. I lifted my drink over my head, channeling all of my years in the service industry, and confidently, sternly started pushing through the crowd. "Drink service, coming through, drink service. Behind!" I could hear my friends doing the same. A whole crew of the most inefficient waitresses you've ever witnessed. But y'all, that shit worked—we made it past the VIP section and got to kick it with Beyoncé. Floored. That's why you always have to operate from the best outcome. If you walk into any room like you're headed for VIP about to have the best night of your life, you just might. Speaking of VIP . . .

SCAM TIP #2: ASK A WHITE MAN

White men have done a lot of shit excellently. Was it good shit? No. Most of it wasn't. But did they do it well? Yes. One of their crowning achievements: systemic racism. That shit is in *EVERYTHING*. You can't get away from it. If I go to a bathroom with an automatic sink, I have to show the white part of my hand to turn it on. Cameras were designed to capture white skin. Don't believe me? Take a Black friend to a photobooth. Don't get me started on how ChatGPT was invented five minutes ago and that bitch is already racist. I'm not saying we should be *like* white men, but I am saying we can *learn* from them. Don't run away from those motherfuckers; that's not the answer. It's important to understand how powerful people gained all that power and how you, a cool and nice person, can learn to also gain power and harness that power for good—or at the very least use it for your own happiness.

A few years ago, I was offered a very exciting opportunity, something that would undeniably change my life, elevate my career, and bring more coin into my bank account. Even though everything within me screamed to accept the offer, I knew I was probably getting the "Happy To Be Here" contract with the "Happy To Be Here" money. "Happy To Be Here" money is what women in creative careers and/or cool jobs get offered. And you know that Black women are getting the worst of it. It's hard to argue your worth when society wants you in the kitchen barefoot and pregnant. It's hard to argue your worth when you're following your calling and there's literally nothing else you'd rather do, know how to do, or want to do. It's hard to argue your worth when you've spent years being made to feel like you're not worth anything. But this doesn't mean that you should shy away from ARGUING YOUR WORTH. Like I've pointed out before, it's easy for people to take advantage of you when you really want something—and I really wanted this job.

Before accepting the offer that I suspected wasn't as good as it could be, I called my friend, a white man, who worked for the same company. I came to the chat ready—notebook, pen, everything. And I asked him straight up, "What are they giving you? Because I want that too. I want the same treatment and the same money." And bless him, he told me everything, because he is a nice dude and nice people do not keep their deal terms a secret. American corporate culture has stigmatized any discussions of money, which makes it harder for the working person to get what they deserve. One of the most valuable things about being in a union is that we communicate and advocate. Companies big and small scam workers out of their worth by intimidating you into keeping salaries and benefits secretive. They are banking on workers not talking to each other because they worry it's rude or inappropriate.

You know why job applications always ask you what's your desired salary range? Because they know you're going to undervalue yourself, especially if it's a job you want in a career you want. If you want to be treated well, to be respected, to get the best deal, don't hesitate to ask someone in the same field, preferably someone with ingrained power ... like a white man ... what they're getting out of the job. If the person you ask doesn't feel comfortable bankrupting their own privilege or sharing a bit of their insider knowledge, then that is not someone you should have in your inner circle—a valuable lesson in and of itself.

SCAM TIP #3:
MAKE LOYALTY YOUR PRIORITY

I have gotten to a point in my career where I am able to hire people. Laci's not only a brand; she's a business, with people on payroll. I run a simple con when it comes to getting the best work out of the people I hire: I am kind to them. I am a kind person, but I also see kindness as an investment. When you're a nice person, pay your employees well, and treat them with respect, they pay you back in loyalty—the most valuable asset out there. I think it's wild that all those old-ass, rich CEOs keep losing their damn minds about what they think is a lack of work ethic among today's labor force. I cannot tell you how many "No one wants to work anymores" I've heard over the past few years. In reality, no one wants to work for *you* (an out-of-touch asshole who doesn't pay well) anymore.

Every time another big, rich fraudster goes down in flames—the Fyre Festival bro, the Theranos lady, the WeWork guy—it all starts with disgruntled employees. Treating my crew with kindness is a calculated business move that I learned from all the times I accidentally worked for mob fronts. Mobsters know how to enterprise right. When a gangster says "you're part of the family," they don't mean it the way startup tech-bro bosses do when they say it to get you to work longer hours—they really mean it. Blood in. Blood out. I value loyalty above all else when it comes to choosing friends, creative partners, employees— because it always pays back dividends. I cannot emphasize enough how much good, kind, compassionate treatment will unlock doors for you. So even when you don't feel like it, choose to be kind. Besides, everyone has a recording machine in their pocket these days and one way or another your business will be brought into the light, so make sure that business is not messy.

SCAM TIP #4:
CRITICIZE WITH "WE" STATEMENTS

Okay, this one is straight-up therapy talk, but sometimes in life, you'll have to set things straight. Conflict can be difficult when you're trying to be a good, kind person. Not everyone is open to criticism, even the constructive kind—so you have to get creative with the way you critique, especially if you want to maintain a reputation that opens doors for you and keeps the people in your orbit loyal and happy.

For years, YEAAAARRRRSSS, I was dealing with makeup artists who didn't know how to enhance Black skin. They would make me look like a faded corpse, and a very big part of my job is *not* looking like a faded corpse, especially on film. In my industry, it's important to maintain good relationships with everyone you work with because you don't want to catch a bad reputation. One twisted rumor can ruin a career: just look at that 27 *Dresses* blonde, who made one mildly sassy statement and didn't get hired for a decade. You also want to stay calm, cool, and collected because crews jump from gig to gig, and there's a very real chance you might work with these people again. I work in a very collaborative space, and since it's so collaborative, it's important to keep the energy fun and light even when you have an understandably frustrating situation like your face is beat like a bat out of hell. Even though I may want to turn to a makeup artist who is struggling with their job and say, "Bitch, you made me, a fine young woman, look like I'm dead. How is my skin gray?!" You can't do that. You have to be kind. I've learned that making it a group activity is more fun for everyone. Instead of saying, "Can *you* fix this?" I say, "Can we fix this lash? Can we warm it up here?" In the battle between criticism and collaboration, collaboration will always win out. In your life, there will be times when people around you genuinely mess up. They do something that makes your life harder or impacts how you do your job or even how you feel about yourself. Regardless of how much you want to whack them upside the head and set them straight for forever, it's better to find a fix together.

SCAM TIP #5:
USE FEWER WORDS

Don't overexplain yourself. It's a bad habit. That's all I'm going to say.

SCAM TIP #6:
BECOME A CONFIDENCE ARTIST

Have you ever asked an airplane pilot to see their credentials? I bet not. You assume a pilot knows how to fly a plane simply because they're sitting in the cockpit. Similarly, most people assume that you know what you're doing when you put yourself in a position to look like you know what you're doing. That's why you need to project confidence. With a strong performance, people really can't tell the difference anyway. Trust me. I'm a professional.

Confidence, conning, being a human . . . it's all just pretend. You know the phrase, "Fake it till you make it"? Well, here's what I've learned: there's no "it" to make. When you get to "it," there will be another "it" up ahead, just out of reach. You have to pretend, always, that you've made it. Some people are naturally confident, and I'm not going to lie to you: I'm one of those people. But even so, I still have doubtful voices in my head that I have to quiet from time to time. Social media (and media-media) has made it seem like success is a solution. This. is. not. true. Everyone who is living the life you wish you had spends some of that life doubting themselves . . . even the confident ones. Next time you hear that doubtful voice in your head, tell that bitch to shut up and keep going about your day. That voice will come back and that's okay. Every time they pull up, kick them out. Remember, confidence is a tool that anyone can use.

SCAM TIP #7:
TAKE YOUR SHIT & TURN IT INTO FERTILIZER

Oooooh, I love this one. Okay, so basically, anything you say or do can be reframed in a positive light, but no one takes the damn time to do it. Like I've said before, every situation should be looked at through multiple perspectives. When I'm choosing the perspective to view something through, I try to go with the most optimistic one.

For example, when you don't know the answer to something or how to do something, it can feel intimidating. People have trouble admitting when they don't know something because they're scared of looking ignorant, which is absurd because we're all ignorant about something . . . No one knows everything. But fine, I get it. You're worried about looking stupid. It's scary! What I do is instead of telling someone, "I don't know how to do this," I find a compliment in my question: "You seem really versed on this, do you mind helping me out?" This is a win-win situation because you get to learn something new without feeling ignorant and you make the person you're talking to feel good enough to open up and share something. You changed the perspective from "I don't know" to "Can you help me?" Asking for, getting, or giving help is always a good thing.

Another example: instead of saying "Sorry, I'm so late," compliment the person with a cute little, "Thank you for your patience." That way, you're not shining a light on your lateness, you're shining a light on their patience. This is basically what ad folk have been doing for decades, putting a positive spin on everything they touch. We all need to tap into that positioning brain from time to time to rework how we talk about ourselves and each other. People seem to forget how much control they have over their own narrative. Showcase yourself and everyone around you in the best light possible, bb—things are so much better that way!

SCAM TIP #8:
WAIT TWO WEEKS

Scammers, especially the ones in it for the long con, are extremely patient people. Playing the long game always works in a con artist's favor because when you are patient, a solution to problems will usually present itself. You just need to keep your eyes and ears open. This is especially useful scamming advice to all my conflict-avoidant girlies. If someone approaches you with an emergency, an opportunity, or a big ask, just wait two weeks. Most things can wait two weeks. People who come to you with a problem can figure out their own shit without you. Even if you're the one causing a problem for yourself, take a breath and wait two weeks. Anxiety and stress always pass; you just have to give it time. It's okay to take your time. "Good things come to those who wait" is a saying for a reason.

SCAM TIP #9:
DON'T BE ASHAMED ABOUT LOSING YOUR SHIT

Okay, remember when I went missing as a five-year-old and Ms. April found me on the side of the road? Remember how, right before that, I was at the leasing office where we lived and I screamed my head off because the person at the desk asked me where my parents were? This moment replays in my head a lot. I wonder where my strength came from. How, at that age, I did not give a fuck when I felt threatened. I just screamed, flapped my arms like a little bird, and got out of the situation. Since that day at the leasing office, I've been in a lot of bad or uncomfortable situations, a lot of which you've read about in this very book. I used to get small and quiet when I was in these situations because I'm a people-pleaser—I don't like it when people are upset with me—but that started to change as I got older, wiser, hotter (i.e., started going to therapy regularly).

Think about it: If someone's breaking into your Honda Accord, the car doesn't go, "Um, excuse me. Sorry to bother you, but can you not do that?" FUCK NO. The car alarm *goes off*. Car alarms are such silly bitches. They're whooping and awoooing, screaming and ringing . . . It's every loud and annoying noise put into one. That's by design to throw off the threat. You never hear a fire alarm like, "Hey, so we think some smoke is happening, you should gather your things and exit the building." The fire alarm is like *AAAAAaaaAAAaaAAAaAAA*. I'm taking a lot of inspo from alarms lately, and my badass five-year-old self. Instead of trying to be polite when you feel like you're being taken advantage of or hurt, become a human fire alarm. Do the weirdest, loudest shit imaginable, flap your arms, scream, and run—chances are you'll freak out any wrongdoers, or at the very least, you'll get away from them. Take it from me: a walking, talking car alarm.

SCAM TIP #10:
DON'T CARE TOO MUCH

My pal and former *Scam Goddess* podcast guest Behzad Dabu once dropped some gems that I still think about to this day. A mentalist, like a real-deal mind-reading sorcerer, gave him this advice: Whether someone's passionate on the side of "I hate this" or passionate on the side of "I love this," it's equally as easy to scam them because they're so invested in their own opinion. The people who are hard to scam are the people who simply don't care. This stuck with me. The con is in the caring. Which is fucked up because it's important to care about things. I care about my family and friends. But I also care about my career, deeply. I care about being liked, too much. I care about how I look, a lot. I'm still learning how to care a little less about the last three things. But at the end of the day, everything good I've gotten in my life is because I care so much. Everything bad that's happened to me is because I care so much. Both can be true. That is just the way of the damn world. Just remember that when you care too much about one thing—a job, a person, an idea—you open yourself up to scammers. So maybe, just maybe, spread out the care a little, so you care a little less and live a little more.

There you have it, some of my favorite scam hacks. Try them out in your day-to-day interactions; they're all yours. I want you to know that it's okay to live life with ulterior motives, to find ways to manipulate the situation in your favor, because that's what everyone is doing whether they admit it or not.

Ultimately, the best con artists out there know the baseline of scamming is all about projecting confidence—even when it's a lie. That's what I want for you: I want you to be more confident and use that confidence to achieve greatness, because if you're reading this book, then I know you're a hot, cool, nice person who deserves all the things. I also know that when you get those things, when you step into your power, you will do good with that power. And hell, maybe you're already standing in your power, I don't know!

CONCLUSION

I've been doing the *Scam Goddess* podcast for a few years now, so I'm *clearly* an expert on all things scam. I've realized that people engage in true con (just like true crime but with less murder!) for two reasons: 1) We're curious. Curiosity is a natural part of the human experience. People get more excited about a thing they've never seen before than something they see every day. 2) We're scared. When people hear about something truly awful, they usually want details—as if those details can provide an answer to how they can avoid having something truly awful happen to them. We, as a collective society, need to focus more on our curiosity and less on our fear. I'm a big believer in "What you pay attention to grows." So let's pay attention to our curiosity.

CURIOSITY CONNED THE CAT

Curiosity is the desire to learn more about the world. I love that for us. But I talk a lot about how desire can open you up to scams. The thing I've always struggled with is finding the solution to that: What is the answer then? To want less? To not be as ambitious? Or as driven? That doesn't seem right. Passion is attractive. You can't stop needing and wanting; the needs and wants are what make you human. Like I've said before, none of us asked to be born, but here we are walking around the world, being all alive and shit. Wanting and needing are part of the whole being-alive thing. We are born wanting and needing. So I'm never going to tell you to quiet those aspects of yourself. Don't run away from your wants and needs; get to know them instead. When you have a clear picture of your desires and how to fuel your curiosity about the world, then you can decipher if the people in your life are preying on those wants *or* providing you with your needs. Telling the difference between those who prey on you and those who provide for you can be a difficult exercise, and that's exactly why you have to examine your own motivations in the world. You have to have a strong understanding of who you are in order to know the people to surround yourself with. People serve different purposes in our lives; it's important to spot that for yourself. Even if you do eventually learn to find the difference between the bad guys and the good guys, that doesn't mean that a few can't slip into your life anyway. They're sneaky motherfuckers, which brings me to my next point.

FEAR & FRAUDING IN LOS ANGELES

Fear is a driving factor in a lot of our obsession with scams. Even if we don't think something horrible will actually happen to us, there's still a little part of our brain that fears it will. It's only natural to get sucked into these stories as a form of self-preservation, as a way to make sure you'd never be caught in the same type of situation. I urge you to let that kind of thinking go. It's these kinds of biases—the feeling that you can rise above horrific mistreatment—that lead you straight into a scam.

Seeing the world of scams not as a matter of *how* but a matter of *when* can be terrifying and depressing. Believe me, I *knooow*. Nothing triggers my depression quite like the understanding that as long as I am a living, breathing human, I will always be vulnerable to getting taken advantage of—but it's also kind of freeing to know there's nothing you can do to prevent yourself from being hurt every now and then. The people who get the worst of it are the ones who believe in absolutes: those who get into religious cults feeling like there's a right path toward salvation, those who get caught up in financial scams believing money is the only security, those who are trapped in romantic scams wanting one partner to sustain them . . . Everything always comes back to the need for an answer. Scams, scammers, and scammy systems prey on our need for salvation, security, safety. The things people see as absolutes in this world—government, laws, rules, societal norms—were created by humans, and not necessarily humans who should've been in charge of their design. Once you allow yourself to accept that you cannot control what happens in this universe, then life will become a little bit easier. When you begin to understand that *anything* can happen to you, then you are truly free and truly protected from the worst ramifications of all the scammy ways of the world.

Everything is made up, so don't be afraid to break the rules. The concept of "breaking the law" sounds intimidating and grandiose by design, but the truth is that laws change all the time, our understanding of how things work is evolving, so you need to evolve too, boo. Make your own rules, make your own laws, and if you don't feel like something is working properly, do it up better. You should live how you want to live as long as your way of living isn't hurting anyone else.

I really believe there should be more good people out in the world running cons. We're all brainwashed into thinking that we should act a certain way to fit into society's definition of what's moral, but it's all bullshit. Being entrenched in the world of fraud has taught me that one of the biggest scams out there is convincing moral people that scamming is bad. If you don't scam your way through life, then getting what you want is going to be pretty difficult. I'm sorry, it just is. The scam of society is that we've made *wanting* things shameful. You're a freelancer and you want money? You are greedy. We shame people out of ambition. You want love? Why are you so thirsty? We shame people out of companionship. There are endless ways in which the people in power are embarrassing us for wanting to live a good life, for having dreams and goals and passions. But, on the flip side, we *let* people embarrass us for wanting things. We, as a culture, have shamed ourselves out of every aspect of being a human being. People have mistaken apathy for strength. But everyone who is not a psychopath cares! Everyone wants!

Having a passion that's so raw it makes you vulnerable to the world is a gift. So stop letting the wealth-hoarders win;

the billionaires, the influencers, yes, even the celebrities—they're all greedy with their accumulation of money, attention, and accolades. You deserve some of that too, and when someone tries to shame you out of it, even if that someone is the media or a social media app or an algorithm or even your own insecurity, tell them to quickly fuck off. There's nothing wrong with wanting, even if that wanting means you might get scammed from time to time.

If you take away one thing from this book, let it be this: **there is no shame in getting scammed**. The reason that the bad scammers keep winning is because they subsist off the shame associated with scamming. That's the only way they can continue doing what they do. That's why one of the first steps to running a successful scam is isolating victims from each other and their own needs. Isolation makes people too socially and emotionally depleted to turn to their community or themselves for help. This is exactly why I started the *Scam Goddess* podcast and why I encourage listeners to write in with their own stories of scams.

SCAM LIFE LESSON

There is no shame in getting scammed.

I want there to be more Scam Goddesses out in the world, more humans who know how to pull the strings of society to make things a little better for themselves and for other people like them. But in order to have the Scam Goddesses win out over the plain old nefarious scammers,

I need you to set aside your shame and share your experiences. If you've been scammed, share it with people. By sharing your story, you can help someone else avoid getting scammed in the same way, or at the very least, you can lighten your load. Guarding your experiences as a shameful thing or a sign of your own foolishness isn't the way to look at the world. Give yourself some grace. Everyone at one point or another gets scammed.

When I first started writing this book, I told y'all it was a scam, and I really believed that. At the time, I felt I had no business writing an actual book. I'd never written a book before! I didn't know what I was doing. But you know who else never wrote a book before they wrote their first book? Every single person who has ever written a book. We all start at the same place: a place of ignorance. It's okay to not know. Instead of feeling ashamed about your lack of understanding, walk toward it.

I've always seen uncharted waters as an opportunity to learn, and what I've learned during the process of writing this book is that when you're uncertain or you don't know how to do something, you have to be vulnerable enough to ask for help. When I first started writing this thing, I had no clue what I was doing, so I turned to my scammer tool kit to get by. I planned for the best outcome, spoke with confidence, and just assumed that a path would open up for me. Sure, sometimes those doubtful voices crept in, but I kept yelling at them to go away and eventually they did. Now that we're here, at the end of this baby, I've realized that I know so much more than the negative voices in my head had been giving me credit for. I've grown stronger and better throughout our journey together. I want to thank you for reading my stories, and I want to thank me for sharing them. Spending even *more* time examining scams—both my own and famous ones from the past—has only made me love them that much more. Like most ambitious and driven humans, I'm constantly looking to self-improve, to do things better, to be happier, healthier, stronger, better, but in writing this book, I've learned that there is no fix. There's no pill or class or filter that you can buy that will magically improve your life. It's all a cycle. Sometimes you're up, sometimes you're down. Nothing is permanent, but that doesn't have to be a bad thing. Instead, see it as an invite to find joy where you can and understand that our definitions of joy can change.

Holding all my experience up to the light and seeing clearly all the wild shit I've done with my thirty-one years is . . . a lot. Like I said, I went into this confidently, expecting the best outcome, but I didn't expect that sharing all of this with you would bring me a stronger sense of self. Compiling all of these experiences into one book, taking a step back and reviewing my past, made me realize that all the shit we go through adds up to a big, messy, funny, difficult story. There's no point in trying to control the story; it's best just to live it and share it. You don't even need to go through the stress of pitching, writing, and promoting a book to solidify your own sense of self: Call a friend and share some deep, dark secrets over wine. Tell a coworker that you need help with something. Bring your little brother to see you in a comedy show. Try pottery. Open your soul up to a new person. Whatever it is, I want to encourage you to get out there and do goofy shit: live a funny, adventurous, vulnerable life. Be overly confident and expect the best outcome, but also give yourself grace when the outcome isn't what you expected. Feel free to change your definition of success, of happiness, of love. Don't shy away from situations that make you feel insecure; dive into them. Stop blocking out the shameful experiences and share them instead. Build community out of your vision of the world. Find the humorous parts of life and uncover the truth within the comedy. Relinquish control and find peace in the chaos.

At the end of the day, the reason I love scammers so much is because they're dreamers. They live in circumstances they don't like in a world they don't love and envision a way to make it a world that they do love and circumstances that they do like. I relate to that. Deeply. I'm a dreamer because a lot of the time I don't like the reality of this world we're living in. And as a dreamer, I spend my days creating things. All these ideas I have in my head are nothing but fantastical frauds until people like you buy into them, and then my fantastical frauds start to change shape and become real, tangible things . . . like this book. Creating something out of nothing is the most incredible and surreal feeling on earth. It's even hard to describe, but I'll try.

A few years ago, I was in my car humming to myself. I'd just sold a show to a major podcast network about my first love: scams. Stuck in traffic on Laurel Canyon, a tune popped in my head, and right after the lyrics followed:

"Scaaaammmmmm, connnnn, robbery, and fraudddd."
So I recorded it on my voice notes. Later that night, I listened to it and thought it was decent enough to share with some people.

Last week, I walked out into a venue packed full of *Scam Goddess* fans and said to them, "If you know it, go on and help me out." The whole sold-out theater burst into the *Scam Goddess* theme song: "Scaaaammmmmm, connnnn, robbery, and fraudddd . . . ." The same song that I had hummed into my iPhone years earlier. Hearing a room full of people sing something that came out of my head is an indescribable experience. It was euphoric. I'm telling you all this because I want you to find your euphoria. I want you to find the thing on this earth that lights up your endorphins and makes you think creatively about living in the world.

Being a creator, a person who makes something out of nothing and then gets paid for that something-nothing, is my biggest con. Standing in a room filled with people who paid their hard-earned money to come watch me duckwalk and tell jokes with my funny friends is heavenly. Like I said at the beginning of this book, I want these experiences for you. I want you to scam your way into *your* fantasies. But in order to turn your dreams into a reality, you're going to have to get creative; you're going to have to work for it; you're going to have to not accept the system as is and dream up what could be.

I've built my brand around being the *Scam **Goddess***. And, yes, I fuck with scams, but I'm also a Goddess. And a

Goddess finds ways to improve the surroundings for everyone while improving her-/him-/themself. I really believe
that all of you can and should be scammers. But I also
believe that all of you can and should be Goddesses/Gods/
Nonbinary Deities, too. So next time you pass through a
gate that's being kept or find a loophole in the broken system or even just learn an easier way to live, a secret code—
share your findings with someone. (I said some*ONE*; don't
put it on TikTok and ruin it for us all.) Life's more fun
that way. Trust me. And always remember, everything is
a scam. lol.

THE END?

Jk. You know I always have more to say.

ACKNOWLEDGMENTS

Who knew being a published author would be my next scam?! I certainly didn't. Writing this book changed my life, and I couldn't have done it without some amazing accomplices.

Marina Shifrin, you put my soul into print. You became my confidante, my therapist, and my friend. You even let me fly to your state and scam my way into your home! Thank you for sharing your light with me. I am forever changed by our time together and your charcuterie boards.

Shannon Kelly, you knew what this book was before I did and you led me to it. Thank you for your guidance and enthusiasm. You're a queen! Thank you to all the great minds who helped make this book happen: Amanda Richmond, Amber Morris, Ashley Benning, Betsy Hulsebosch, Cindy Sipala, Elizabeth Parks, Jack Smyth, Jenn Kosek, Jess Riordan, Kara Thornton, Kristin Kiser, Sara Puppala, Susan Eberhart, and everyone at Hachette Book Group.

Cindy Uh, your dedication is unmatched. I appreciate all the Zoom calls, even from your car! Emily. EMILY JONES!!!!! I wouldn't be here without you. This book wouldn't be here without YOU. Everyone who meets you always has the most wonderful things to say after. You have changed my life for the better, lifted my spirit, and bumped every email to the heavens! You are truly one of the most gifted people I have ever met, an icon in the making, and I am honored to have worked with you. Thank you, Emily.

Thank you to my support system: Johanna Joseph, Chereen Pasha, Courtney Jones, Anthony Simpson, Sydnee Washington, Mary Anthony, Edgar Momplaisir, Jojo T. Gibbs Leroy, Ruha Taslimi, Emile Ennis, and John Filizzola. I love you all so much. Shout out to my English teachers who let me bother them from youth to adulthood, Erin Jewell and Belinda Nolan. Grace Kallis, you are my guiding light; Josh Lieberman, you are the wind beneath my wings; Katie Newman, you are my rock; thank you all so much!!! Colin Anderson, thank you for giving my lil podcast a chance when I just had a tiny scam résumé and a dream. Your kindness and belief in me are something I cherish every single day. Thank you Punkie Johnson.

CONAN O'BRIEN!!! My redheaded king!!! You gave me my first late-night spot!!! The fact that I had to do it in my car while stealing Wi-Fi from a café solidified my confidence as a scammer. You are so funny and kind and I'm honored to work with you. Thank you so much for seeing me; it means the world!

JUDITH!!! Judith Kargbo!! My podcast producing queen! *Scam Goddess* wouldn't be here without you! Thank you so much for being the best in the game. Kaelyn Brandt, you are stellar and I'm so blessed to work with you. Earwolf, Sirius XM, Team Coco, Sharilyn Vera, Cody Ziglar, Codi

Fischer, Sam Kieffer, and Abby Aguilar. Miles Gray, you started calling me Scam Goddess as a joke and it just stuck with me. You're one of the realest in the business. I'm so happy to know you. Thank you, king! Anna Hossnieh, you scammed me into a podcast career all those years ago and I will always be grateful to you for that and so much more! Jack O'Brien, you are my original podcast father. Thank you for teaching me this world!

CONgregation, I love you so much!! I love your letters where you snitch on yourselves and your friends and family. I love meeting you at my live shows. I love chatting with you online. I love our parasocial relationship. Thank you for listening to my nonsense and sharing it with your friends. Thank you for keeping me sane during the dark times. Thank you for sending me so much love and positivity. Thank you for scamming.

Laura Chinn, you gave me my first acting job and we both know I scammed my way in! Thank you for guiding me, for loving me, for being such a wonderful friend. You give the best hugs and I feel lighter every time I see you. You are a gift to this world and to me. I love you.

Hey, family! Eric Mosley, thank you for being my first best friend and role model. I love you so much. Lori, Clarence, Isaac, Constance, aka Moms & Dads, your support means the world!! I wouldn't be anywhere without you, and I thank you all from the bottom of my heart! Josh, Taylor, Syd, I love you. Okay, I wrote a book, y'all! Thank you!!!

SELECTED SOURCES
AND FURTHER READING

RELIGIOUS SCAMS:
GOD, GIVING, AND GUCCI

Gonen, Yoav, and George Joseph. "Brooklyn Pastor Pleads
for Sympathy in Wake of Sermon Robbery, Won't
Discuss Debts." The City, July 31, 2022. https://
www.thecity.nyc/brooklyn/2022/7/29/23284458
/brooklyn-pastor-lamor-whitehead-pleads-for-sympathy.

Korab, Alek. "Gucci-Loving Robbed Pastor's 'Wild' Life Revealed."
Newsful, August 5, 2022. https://bestlifeonline.com
/news-robbed-pastor-whitehead-life-details/.

Velsey, Kim. "Bishop Lamor Whitehead Owns a Lot of Real Estate.
Or Does He?" Curbed, July 29, 2022. https://www.curbed
.com/2022/07/bishop-lamor-whitehead-real-estate-holdings
-default.html.

Wilson, Michael. "ID Theft, Fraud, Prison: The Wild Life of a Bishop
Robbed at the Pulpit." New York Times, August 4, 2022. https://
www.nytimes.com/2022/08/04/nyregion/lamor-whitehead
-bishop-robbed.html.

JOB SCAMS:
THE SILICON VALLEY THEFT BRO

Associated Press. "How an Alabama City Fell for a Massive, $1.9
Million Scam." AL.com, February 26, 2019. https://www.al.com
/news/2019/02/how-an-alabama-city-fell-for-a-massive-19
-million-scam.html.

———. "Kyle Sandler Explains How He Conned Opelika Out of $1.9 Million on HBO's 'Generation Hustle.'" AL.com, May 3, 2021. https://www.al.com/news/2021/05/kyle-sandler -explains-how-he-conned-opelika-out-of-19-million-on-hbos -generation-hustle.html.

Beahm, Anna. "Auburn Man Pleads Guilty to Defrauding $1.8 Million from Investors." AL.com, August 22, 2018. https://www .al.com/news/2018/08/auburn_man_pleads_guilty_to_de.html.

Brown, Melissa. "Alabama Tech Scammer Sentenced to over 5 Years in Prison." *Montgomery Advertiser*, March 26, 2019. https://www .montgomeryadvertiser.com/story/news/crime/2019/03/26 /lee-county-roundhouse-founder-kyle-sandler-sentenced -prison/3279308002/.

Thornton, William. "Kyle Sandler, John McAfee Associate Who Scammed Alabama Town Out of $1.9 Million, Featured on HBO's Generation Hustle." AL.com, April 23, 2021. https://www .al.com/news/birmingham/2021/04/kyle-sandler-john-mcafee -associate-who-scammed-alabama-town-out-of-19-million -featured-on-hbos-generation-hustle.html.

HOUSING SCAMS: QUEENS OF THE CON

Annese, John. "Scam Artist Queens Clan Ran 'One-Family Crime Spree,' Stole Dead Man's $700,000 House: D.A." *New York Daily News*, May 5, 2022. https://www.nydailynews.com/2022/05/04 /scam-artist-queens-clan-ran-one-family-crime-spree-stole -dead-mans-700000-house-da/.

DeGregory, Priscilla. "Family Trio Charged in Scams, Including Stealing $700K House from Dead Man." *New York Post*, May 4, 2022. https://nypost.com/2022/05/04/nyc-family-trio-charged -in-stealing-700k-house-from-dead-man/.

"NYC Family of Con Artists Charged with Litany of Crimes for Decade-Long Scams: DA." NBC New York, May 4, 2022. https:// www.nbcnewyork.com/news/local/crime-and-courts/nyc -family-of-scam-artists-charged-with-litany-of-crimes-for -decade-long-schemes-da/3674285/.

SUCCESS SCAMS: SHONDA CRIMES

Kaplan, Michael, and Joshua Rhett Miller. "Pals of 'Grey's Anatomy' Cancer-Faker Elisabeth Finch Reveal Even More of Her Sick, Lying Ways." *New York Post*, December 13, 2022. https://nypost.com/2022/12/12/elisabeth-finchs-pals-reveal-lies-by-greys-anatomy-writer/.

Kiefer, Peter. "The 'Grey's Anatomy' Liar Confesses It All." The Ankler., December 7, 2022. https://theankler.com/p/the-greys-anatomy-liar-confesses.

Rice, Lynette. "Former 'Grey's Anatomy' Writer Elisabeth Finch Admits 'I've Never Had Any Form of Cancer' in New Interview." Deadline, December 8, 2022. https://deadline.com/2022/12/former-greys-anatomy-writer-elisabeth-finch-never-had-cancer-new-interview-1235192354/.

FRIENDSHIP SCAMS:
THE BAD BITCH OF BUNKER HILL

Kilkenny, Katie. "The Hollywood Producer, the 'Heiress' and a Very Personal Quest for Justice." *Hollywood Reporter*, September 16, 2021. https://www.hollywoodreporter.com/features/hollywood-producer-heiress-a-very-personal-quest-justice-1278611.

FAMILIAL SCAMS:
KEEPING UP WITH THE JOHNSES

"Brother and Sister Charged with Cryptocurrency Fraud in New York." *Guardian*, March 8, 2022. https://www.theguardian.com/technology/2022/mar/08/john-jonatina-barksdale-cryptocurrency-charges-ormeus-coin-new-york.

"SEC Obtains Judgment Against Siblings Who Orchestrated Massive Crypto Asset Fraud." U.S. Securities and Exchange Commission, March 30, 2023. https://www.sec.gov/litigation/litreleases/lr-25680.

Stempel, Jonathan. "U.S. Charges Two Siblings in $124 Million Cryptocurrency Fraud." Reuters, March 8, 2022. https://www.reuters.com/article/us-usa-crime-crypto-currency-barksdale-idCAKBN2L52IZ.

ROMANCE SCAMS: DR. DUPE

Ciralsky, Adam. "The Celebrity Surgeon Who Used Love, Money, and the Pope to Scam an NBC News Producer." *Vanity Fair*, January 5, 2016. https://www.vanityfair.com/news/2016/01/celebrity-surgeon-nbc-news-producer-scam.

Rasko, John, and Carl Power. "Dr Con Man: The Rise and Fall of a Celebrity Scientist Who Fooled Almost Everyone." *Guardian*, September 1, 2017. https://www.theguardian.com/science/2017/sep/01/paolo-macchiarini-scientist-surgeon-rise-and-fall.